FOLKLORE
for the time of your life

Folklore
for the time of your life

Elaine S. Katz

OXMOOR HOUSE, INC. · BIRMINGHAM

Library of Congress Catalog Number: 78-55773
ISBN: 0-8487-0488-6

Manufactured in the United States of America

First Printing

FOLKLORE For the Time of Your Life

Editors: *Ann H. Harvey*
Karen Phillips Irons

Photo Credits, Title Page: Courtesy of
Choctaw Community News, Philadel-
phia, Mississippi, and the *Southern
Living* Photography Staff

"Fa Sol La" by Jerry House. Copy-
right© 1973, Sawgrass Music Publish-
ers, Inc., Nashville.

For George

2036246

Acknowledgments

First, I am deeply indebted to Sam B. Girgus for launching me into folklore; then to James M. Salem for lending a helping hand before I was able to paddle my own canoe; and perennially to Reid Badger for his counsel and support.

Thanks to the generosity of Joe Goodwin, Tina Hammon, Cindy McMillian, Karen Beth Mael, Sandy Lindemann, Jim Salem, Ilse and Davin Schoenberger, Bob Sepe, and James Walker, I had only to ask in order to receive expertise, information, or services of considerable assistance to the completion of my work.

I am grateful to all the kids in Klickie Thornton's fourth, fifth, and sixth grade classes for letting me record thirty-five miles' worth of their folk songs during a Tuscaloosa County Schools excursion. I am particularly indebted to author Jan Harold Brunvand's 1968 edition of *The Study of American Folklore* and to editor Wayland D. Hand's two-volume *Popular Beliefs and Superstitions from North Carolina* for providing the cornerstones of the collectors' classification outline in the Appendix.

The following one-time University of Alabama students deserve credit for collecting some of the illustrative short forms of verbal lore presented in the chapter, "Be Your Own Folklore Resource": Susan Brown, David Carroll, John R. Cook, Georgia Day, Grady E. Downey, Jr., Stephen Eberhart, Edward Journey, James Layton, Sandy Lusk, David Meginniss, Rod K. Nelson, Kitty Taber, Norma Thompson, James A. Turberville, Paul Weeks, Jean Wilson, and Jennifer Wilson.

The unqualified devotion of my husband, to whom this book is dedicated, can never be adequately acknowledged or repaid. Nor can the generosity of my children, Teddy, Caroline, and Jonathan. My family sacrificed their rightful claims on my time and contributed all of theirs toward my well-being and that of our household during the preparation of this manuscript.

My heart and gratitude belong to all the wonderful folks who agreed to serve as informants for the demonstration interviews. These good people are the soul of this book and, indeed, represent the best reasons why folklore collecting is for the time of one's life. It is my hope that they will continue to reckon their unreserved friendship, trust, hospitality, and donations of time and effort as well spent.

Contents

Give a man a fish and he eats for a day.
Teach a man to fish and he eats for a lifetime.

Introduction

Folklore is more than dulcimers in Kentucky or mule trading in Tennessee or sorghum mills in Mississippi or white oak split baskets in Alabama or all-day Fa Sol La singings in Georgia, though it is all these things. It is also Grandmother's childhood reminiscences, kid brother's riddle jokes and parody songs, Aunt Martha's original quilt pattern and method for drying fruit, Uncle Ed's shaggy dog stories, everybody's favorite theory on how to cure the hiccoughs, Mom's cooking prior to monosodium glutamate or red food coloring, and Dad's army songs (if you can get him to sing them for you in their unexpurgated versions).

The emphatically human values inherent in American folk traditions—values born of struggle during times consistently more hard than easy—appeal to high-, low-, and middlebrows in common. Like grass, whose roots can manage to find sustenance between the tiniest crevices in concrete, folklore thrives everywhere, not just among the elderly or in remote rural settings.

The American landscape has become dotted with seasonal folk arts and music festivals. Whether these occur—like the annual National Folk Festival at Wolf Trap in Vienna, Virginia, in a scenic park—like the Smithsonian Institution's National Folklife Festival on the Washington, DC Mall—or even like many a merchant-sponsored crafts show in a suburban shopping mall, enthusiastic crowds flock to the public performances of traditional music, the demonstrations of skills indigenous to regional or ethnic groups, and the sales of handcrafted wares. Not since the days of their necessity, that is, before industrialization in America, have traditional handicrafts enjoyed such demand. Vacationing families can devote entire holidays to making the circuit of crafts fairs, fiddlers' conventions, or even native American powwows.

However, it is not necessary to leave home or to seek out special occasions to become exposed to American folk traditions. From the graffiti-studded walls of the subway station to the teenagers' hamburger hangout, the truck stop to the college campus, the factory to the church hall, folklore circulates wherever people share interests—interests most likely born of region, occupation, religion, ethnicity, or age. Nor should those of us without occasion to have mastered performing arts or traditional manual skills consider ourselves on the outside looking in.

Most of us have not learned from a grandfather how to saddle-notch (or U-notch) the logs for a corncrib. Your father might not have needed to know how to call hogs one way and cows another in syllables so crisp and loud that only his and not his neighbors' would come a-running from two miles in any direction. Your mother or grandmother may not have shown you how to piece a "Grandmother's Flower Garden" or "Log Cabin" quilt top; nor may she have passed on to you the formula for that rural mainstay of the Depression days, a one-two-three-four cake (one cup of butter, two cups of sugar, three cups of flour, and four eggs). All the same, we each possess a legacy of folk traditions, however rich or modest, though it may be stored out-of-awareness.

The traditional definition of a pessimist as a person who pronounces half-empty the same kettle of fish that the optimist observes to be half-full applies here. For, even within earshot of the valid urgings that there is no time to lose in recording the folk traditions, preserving the skills, and documenting the artifacts which are fast disappearing from the American scene, we need also to remind ourselves that the rootage of folklore continually sprouts new growth—like the modern joke with its formularized opening, "Have you heard the one about," which has the same roots as the traditional folktale that begins "once upon a time." Every man, woman, and child is the bearer and disseminator of some folk traditions.

For ordinary folks who take pleasure in their grassroots traditions, it is one kind of experience to study the well-documented collections made by folklore scholars, still another to walk through a museum of folklife, and another again to clap to the music from one's seat in the audience at a folk festival. If passive appreciation does not fully satisfy the hunger for direct involvement in America's most revealing mode of cultural expression, then let us consider participating in the harvest. Why should we not become folklorists ourselves and, in the bargain, enter an exhilarating new dimension in self-discovery?

Just as tracing our ancestry, our personal roots, heightens our sense of identity to include kinship, so nurturing and harvesting our cultural grass roots broadens our sense of kinship to include community. But a tree is distinctly defined within its own space while grass ranges beyond personal property lines. When mowing or raking, we can't always tell where our own turf leaves off and our neighbor's begins.

For the folklorist the idea of continuity is so real it can almost be folded up and put in one's pocket. Unvarnished reality, moreover, is the stuff of folklore—communication through word, song, gesture, deed, or artifact of people when they are being most unself-consciously themselves. That is why collecting folklore makes us feel wholly human. The present book is thus concerned with providing tips on harvesting grass roots (your own and your neighbors'), and on retrieving folk traditions perhaps long stored in the memory. It is concerned with triggering responses to surroundings by means of which anyone can be active as a folklorist.

Collecting folklore is tremendous fun. It engages the intellect and all our senses, together with their extensions—the notebook, tape recorder, and camera. Getting high on grass roots can be habit-forming and contributory to a general sense of well-being. Side effects include heightened powers of observation, a growing tolerance for human foibles, an increased appetite for humor, and a compulsive desire to listen very carefully to others. Once turned on to folklore, an individual is usually "hooked for good" and liable to produce collections long to be treasured by family members or even an entire community.

To become familiar with the range of folklore and to acquire a few basic skills for recording and organizing its messages is to become a person upon whom nothing is lost, to encounter the grand in the familiar and the familiar in the alien. Collecting folklore can turn daily routine into high adventure. It cements friendships with relatives no longer taken for granted, puts travelers at ease among strangers, and can transform new acquaintances into adopted families.

Encounters with the folk—our own folks, as we call our families, or resource contacts less familiar to us—allow us free movement across social, educational, economic, or regional boundaries. The folklorist is privileged to gain access to the human heart. The illustrative examples in this book have been gathered primarily from a Southern field of experience. But wherever the compass points you to, there's harvesting to be done. And whether your turf is alfalfa or asphalt, you're in for the time of your life.

Harvesting Grass Roots:
What It's All About

What Is Folklore Anyway?

Folklore is whatever people say and do when they are being most comfortably themselves. That's essentially it, distilled and poured into a nutshell. But like most boiled down information, and quite unlike a jigger of good Kentucky bourbon, this "quick one" isn't going to warm your heart or give you cheer until you become familiar with the ingredients prior to their distillation.

The term *folk* translates into people, usually within groups. And *lore* is the informally acquired and passed along know-how that people in folk groups share in common. *Folklore* then refers to our informal ways of saying, believing, behaving, working, making, singing, and playing. It refers to all the customary ways (folkways), and sometimes to the very life-styles (folklife) through which we experience and express what is most culturally fundamental to us—that which sprouts from our grass roots.

Whether we pronounce it, tell it, sing it, play it, or make it happen by using our hands; whether we do it out of need for practical solutions to immediate problems or for entertainment or aesthetic pleasure, folklore is all the good stuff we know that we never had to learn in school but picked up from each other by hearing, watching, trying it out, and passing it on, often without even thinking about it twice. It's doing what comes naturally—not because it's in our genes but because it's part of the cultural air we breathe, our traditional environment. Our informal traditions, our cultural grassroots heritage, even our down-to-earthiness are to be regarded by all of us as something in which to take great pride and pleasure—something to nurture, harvest, and carefully preserve.

Folklore happens to be all around us, everywhere. But that does not mean to imply that everything in our environment is necessarily folklore. So, before you can collect it, either as you find it or selectively—from so wide a range of specialties that the lore of beekeepers, bottle diggers, bus drivers, and bottleneck guitar bluesmen scarcely makes a dent in the possibilities under *B* alone—you must be able to recognize it where you find it.

Cultural Patterns: Elite, Pop, Folk

For most of us the total cultural environment manifests three dominant patterns of experience: elite, popular, and folk. Although these three kinds of human environments are commonly described in terms of levels, with elite at the top and folk at the bottom, it is more accurate to view them as intersecting, even overlapping. For, at the same time that each exists in its own right and with equal validity, each touches and interacts with the others.

How do you recognize folk culture? It's simple; you just do like Ed Cress of Kentucky. He's known exactly how to carve an owl ever since the day he realized that you merely whittle away everything from a block of wood that's *not* an owl! In other words, a good way to carve out an understanding of the shape of folk cultural traditions is to mentally whittle away at the whole cultural block until the patterns which are not folk have been eliminated and the patterns which are take on a clearly discernible shape.

Rural, agrarian, or peasant culture was the norm in preindustrial society. While folk culture thus has its origins in rural settings, present-day folk groups tend to form in all communities, including urban, and our grassroots traditions may spread to any type of environment. This is exemplified in the experience of rural Mississippi-born Robert Billie, oldest of eight Choctaw children. Because jobs were scarce in Pearl River, his father moved the family to Chicago, where Robert grew up speaking Choctaw as well as English. Moreover, as he remembers, *There were other Indians there—Sioux, Cheyennes, Navahos, Apaches—and we learned their songs.* Folk groups formed, and relocated traditions continued to circulate because of *annual powwows in the Chicago Armory Center and because many of them lived in the same city neighborhoods.*

Transplanted members of regional or ethnic folk groups tend to form "cultural islands" in the city, where new customs will eventually take hold but many of the old ones remain in practice nonetheless. While most urban folk traditions have nonurban roots, city folklife can generate its own informal traditions, such as the ritual painting of class "signatures" on strategically located viaducts by groups of graduating high school seniors.

The wellsprings of elite culture are in urban areas, where cathedrals, academies, conservatories, museums, universities, and theaters function as centers for its preservation and maintenance. Elite lore is formally acquired and transmitted by "the select few." Membership in elite circles is based on accomplishments as diverse as being a collector of scarce European wines, writing a doctoral dissertation on medieval Spanish poetry, or owning a perfectly cut emerald.

In folk culture, the impulse toward originality is superseded by an appetite for the basic fare of tradition, informally maintained by group consensus. Traditions are patterns of repetition. They are optionally repeated ways of doing things. The older ways are chosen despite existing alternatives; whatever the reason, they are considered worth maintaining.

Elite culture also feeds on traditions, but these are formally maintained in relatively unvarying texts; quite literally, as in the printed scores from which "longhaired music" is performed; even figuratively, as in the formalities attendant upon a young woman's social debut. Elite culture, print-oriented since the invention of movable type, has always been literary. On the other hand, pop culture, the child of modern technology, is disseminated by means of all the mass communications media, including print. Wherever there are newspapers, billboards, drugstores, brand-name products, pop culture is expressing itself, and we are interacting with it. The life blood of folklore, however, circulates mainly orally. With only a few exceptions—such as the broadside ballads of a bygone

era, modern "droodles," or the ever-traditional epitaphs (tombstone inscriptions), flyleaf inscriptions, autograph rhymes, and
graffiti—folk culture has always been characteristically nonliterary.

What's this? 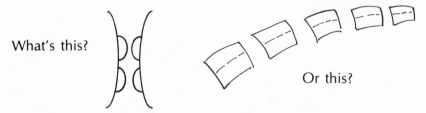   Or this?

Here are two well-known examples of "droodles," which are drawn or doo-
dled on note pads to provide informal folk group entertainment. Much like
the riddler, a droodler will ask, "Guess what this is?" fully expecting to
provide the answer as a humorous surprise as soon as you say, "I give up."
The classic picture riddles scribbled above are traditionally identified (from
left to right) as a bear climbing a tree and a highway for grasshoppers. You'll
probably recall lots more.

Where the Elite and Folk May Meet: Mozart lovers need not be
mansion dwellers any more than ballad singers have to hail from the
boondocks. Elite culture is not so exclusive that it cannot overlap
with folk culture in some interesting ways, as revealed in the career
of Robert Griffith, a blacksmith with a university degree in fine art.

Bob Griffith's situation is nontraditional. The first "artist craftsman" in his city to open a studio workshop sponsored by a nonprofit
corporation, his occupation combines the informally acquired skills
of the American blacksmith with the creativity of the artist formally
trained in research as well as design. Even while he must answer to
the corporate business world where time is money, he also strives to
maintain the spirit of the traditional artisan operating on informal
time, gladly sharing some of the latter with a folklore collector.

At his Black Warrior Forge, so called because blacksmiths
traditionally named their forges after nearby rivers, Griffith makes
iron artifacts by hand for customers with special needs or just a
special love for historical reproductions. He's most interested in
*things like the folding knife which I sold to a museum in North
Carolina, and a pastry tool I've got in the Smithsonian collection. Everything I do has a function. That's why I consider
myself a craftsman and not an artist.*

Watching Bob at work, with a handkerchief over one's nose in a feeble attempt to filter out the acrid odors of coal fire and smoke, or inspecting the wrought iron folk artifacts on display at the front of his Quonset hut workshop, one begins to realize just how many and how various were the demands that had to be met by early

Marshal Hagler

Blacksmith Robert Griffith is at the anvil "hammer-welding a billet," one of many steps prior to forging a "skelp" to its proper size. With the heat from the forge, the power from the trip hammer, and the support of the anvil, the smith begins to "run out sixteen feet to do a thirty-inch gun barrel." The billet is then cut and restacked: "If I want sixteen layers, I'll cut and stack four at a time. The billet is always the same size, but I'll hammer it out again to end up with more stacked layers. So it's the same size, only thinner layers each time."

community blacksmiths—demands besides those for horseshoes and farm implements, for the useful as well as the decorative.

On display at the forge are gun barrels, andirons, door latches and door knockers, trunk hinges and keys, candle holders, weather vanes, and kitchen utensils like trivets and pastry tools. And there is an assortment of blades and picks for every traditional purpose from chopping, paring, and carving wood or food, to hunting man or beast, to self-defense in warfare or civilian life.

Bob points out a push dagger like those once used by riverboat gamblers: *They could tuck it neatly in their vest, and use it in a tight situation.* He recalls the weather vane he once wrought *for a group of old Indian believers that had a secret society.* It had the letters T-O-T-E worked into it. *T-O-T-E stood for something*

At the Black Warrior Forge, Robert Griffith fashions such iron artifacts, along with their polished wooden handles, as (clockwise from top) a reproduction of an eighteenth-century Pennsylvania Dutch trivet, a hunting knife, pastry 'jig' or pie crimper, food chopper, and push dagger. He also wrought the coal shovel shown resting in its usual place on the forge.

sacred, but they told everybody it meant "too old to eat."

He picks up a section of gun barrel and begins to explain how Damascus steel is forged, pointing out the wavy lines, resembling wood grain, that result from the refining method used:

All these lines that you see are layers of iron and steel that have been hammered together. It's one I made last year, and we're now doing one that'll be thirty-two inches long. This will get about three to four hundred heats in the forge and probably over a million hammer blows before it's all done. It's for a fifty-four caliber muzzleloader, a reproduction of a 1680s wheel lock model that'll be mounted on a rifle by a gunsmith in North Carolina.

I'll be laminating the pieces of iron and steel into what's called a skelp. See this shotgun barrel? We're using the same technique. These three bars right here have sixteen layers of iron and steel. They're twisted and then hammer-welded together into the skelp. And then that skelp is wrapped in a helix around this core from one end to the other and then heated up in the forge. And that whole mass is welded together. That's what gives you your finished barrel.

In the old days they did not have refined steels like they do today. So they refined it themselves by combining very precious carbon steel with not-so-precious wrought iron and began developing patterns into the bargain—similarly to what the Japanese do with Samurai swords. This process was used for gun barrels up until the turn of this century. It hasn't been used since then.

Pop Is All Around: For Bob Griffith, the researcher-blacksmith, elite and folk environments consistently interact. But it could never be said that elite culture daily affects all Americans. Most of us at least touch base with folk culture daily—if only by reason of its persistence in casual speech. But no matter where we live or how we live, none of us are exempt from the myriad, round-the-clock influences of popular culture.

Visit the Choctaw community, a cultural island steeped in native traditions, near Philadelphia, Mississippi, and you may come upon traditionally clothed women pounding hominy with a heavy stick in a hollowed out walnut stump, to the rhythmical beat of radioed-in rock music.

Choctaw folkways blend with pop culture: In keeping with folk tradition, Willie B. Willis pounds the husks off the hominy, a Choctaw staple. Her domestic chore, like those of American householders everywhere, seems to go better to piped-in rock music.

While elite culture appeals selectively, and folk cultural expressions are indigenous to interest groups, manifestations of pop culture—from digital mini computers to jeans—are, in a word, ubiquitous. The mainspring of popular culture is free enterprise. Aimed at once at factory town, farming community, ghetto tenement, or suburban estate, pop culture constitutes the sum total effects of what is developed in the marketplace by means of mass production, packaging, and promotion.

Products of pop culture appeal to the common denominator—our eagerness for convenience, ease, and expedience. Popular culture would starve without a constant flow of fresh but often short-lived, trend-setting ideas. The pop cultural artifact is instant

Marshal Hagler

The dogtrot house, prevalent in the deep South from around 1800 to 1920, was formed when a second "single pen" log house was constructed on the gable side of a first. The addition was placed from ten to twelve feet away from the earlier built structure, though the two were joined at the roof. The resultant breezeway or "dogtrot" provided a modicum of relief from the heat of Southern summers. It thus became the center of whatever household activities—from pea shelling to storytelling—could be performed there during warm weather.

Marshal Hagler

Staying Power: Half-dovetail notching, prevalent in Piedmont folk building.

and disposable, quickly manufactured and consumed, then obsolete. Its purpose is to be used up, tossed out, or traded in, and it is fad-oriented.

Expressions of folk culture, however, lack novelty that quickly wears thin. Folk artifacts have great staying power, like the Kentucky mountain ballads which go back as far as the British middle ages, or the termite-free logs—perhaps hewn to a plank shape and half-dovetail cornered—of a second generation dogtrot folk house.

Contrast the groans in response to such worn-out utterances as "gee, that's swell!" or "groovy!" with the appreciative reception and vigorous use given hundreds of folk sayings generations old, like "a stitch in time saves nine" and "haste makes waste."

In folklife, little indeed is wasted and less is thrown away. Be it logs or hogs, the old saw about using all but the squeal is well nigh literally true. Elvin King of Sewanee, Tennessee, who skillfully combines modern technology and an old-fashioned craft by doing his whittling with a chain saw, is characteristically thrifty with wood.

Marshal Hagler

When we got the small wood, I do some little stuff. Take a little rim about the size of your little finger, and make a little bird and a little mushroom out of it. I don't want to see anything waste. When I was cutting timber, I used to worry about all that

Marshal Hagler

Chain Saw King: At any crafts fair he attends, Elvin King of Sewanee, Tennessee, will have the loudest demonstration area and the most crowded. He draws spectators like bees to honey, only it's Mr. King who does the buzzing as he carves a graceful wooden duck—with a chain saw. His wife, Barbara, laughingly confides that someone came all the way from Louisiana to Fort Deposit, Alabama, to see her husband peel an apple. "We come down one time to Montgomery, and that's all we done all day long. They wanted to show it on the news."

I was leaving in the woods. You cut a couple of logs off and then you leave more than you really took of the real good wood.

So now, Mr. King goes looking for walnut stumps to dig up and carve into dough bowls or beautiful wooden turkeys or wild ducks.

Distinguishing Characteristics of Folklore

No less than pounding hominy to pop music, carrying on the family tradition of quilting while viewing TV soap operas or picking up new licks and fiddle tunes from country music programming is simply an activity performed in overlapping cultural environments. But because nobody doesn't like folklore, it is sometimes "invented" to help sell merchandise.

The giant lumberjack on TV who can't seem to get enough of his mother's commercially frozen biscuits is not a folk character. Neither is the lovable, quite long-lived Jolly Green Giant, who suggests both a mythical vegetation deity and—by his "ho! ho! ho!"—the kindly giver of good things, Santa Claus. Manufactured folklore belongs fully to pop culture, which, of course, has every right to it, just as collectors have to the real McCoy.

Genuine folklore is neither better nor worse, more joyous nor sad, more fastidious nor crude, more considerate nor rude than the attitudes of its human disseminators. Earthy language, off-color anecdotes, even obscenities and cruel remarks are as much part and parcel of folk culture, indeed of life itself, as good-natured wit and teasing, harmless practical jokes, and fun-loving pastimes.

One example of folk humor illustrates both sides of this coin, depending on the context of its utterance: "How many _____s does it take to change a light bulb?" "One to hold it and five to turn the ladder." The target varies so considerably in this widely circulated slur that scarcely a national, ethnic, regional, or occupational group is exempt—and certainly no rival football fan is.

Happenings in pop culture appear to burst forth spontaneously but derive from the collaborative efforts of many minds and pocketbooks. Never consciously planned as a thing apart, folklore evolves organically out of the life of a community. Folk customs, often born of hard times—economic or social—develop to satisfy a practical need, the craving for beauty, or any other human motive whose informal expression is acceptable within the folk group. The latter can be as large as an entire community, as small as one's own family.

Variations on the tried and true are the spice of folklife. Ask yourself, for example, how many sets of lyrics you can remember hearing or singing yourself to the melody of "The Old Grey Mare" or to that of "The Battle Hymn of the Republic." In like manner, traditional mountain dulcimers have hourglass or teardrop shapes; they come with three strings or four strings. As all quilters know, even if just the color combination of the pieces is varied, no two quilts will look alike, no matter how many times the same pattern of geometric shapes is used.

Quilting lore collected from Mrs. Lois Dodson of Mountain View, Arkansas, attests to several types of variation—in naming practices, in structure, in materials—that are legitimately found to occur in almost any form of folk cultural expression:

A lot of patterns in different localities are known by different names. I used to think that at least the "Grandmother's Flower Garden" was pretty universally known by that name. But so many people come in and call it "The Garden Walk," and "French Bouquet," and "Rose Garden." I hadn't realized before that it was ever known by anything else than "Flower Garden."

Most of your fabrics today are good, washable fabrics, although you don't hardly get one-hundred percent cotton in sheets now. I guess the "Log Cabin" is the older pattern than the "Flower Garden" and the "Double Wedding Ring." It utilizes more of the kinds of fabrics they had a long time ago.

Now, in this "Double Wedding Ring," they would almost have to go out and buy some fabric for this white background. There was a time when they didn't do that. And the "Flower Garden" is a little bit wasteful. These patterns came along, I think, after we had lived a little more affluently than we did in the days of the "Log Cabin."

They used to make the "Log Cabin" quilts where every piece was not uniform like we make them now. They would piece

*them just to keep all the light on one side of the block and all
the dark on the other side. They might not necessarily have
made their strips to be the same width, so they could make use
of everything they had.*

Perpetually dynamic, the folk item sometimes shifts its alle-
giance—wholly or partially—to a pop cultural environment. The
transfer can be permanent or temporary. Popularity could have
resulted in quick-freezing the ballad "Tom Dooley," when the
Kingston Trio made a widely enjoyed, soon forgotten hit recording
of it in the fifties. Yet to this day, "Tom Dooley" continues its life as
a narrative folk song, varying in its music and lyrics from singer to
singer.

Folklore changes with the times. In the South folks used to "stamp
mules" for luck. If they spotted a white mule, they'd lick the palm of
the right hand, clap the wet spot against the left palm, and "stamp"
the left palm with a right closed fist. By the time mule-drawn wagons
had become an oddity on municipal roads, folks were stamping
grey mules. Nowadays, urban Southerners, who could go a lifetime
without setting eyes on a mule, like to perform the stamping gesture
when they spot a red Volkswagen.

Folklore is exciting to collect because it's an inexhaustible field.
You can collect repeatedly from the same person, and you can
collect from an unlimited array of topics. You can specialize
narrowly or broadly, in crafts, for instance, or just in basketry lore.
One of our most highly prized American folk traditions is the music
that has evolved into the blues.

Irrespectively of stylistic origins (for controversy abounds on that
question), the situational origins of the Negro blues, like the field
hollers that preceded, are hard times, hard work, and often social
rejection. Not for sentimentalizing are the fear of death, sweat of
fatigue, loss of individual or cultural integrity. But these motives as
much as those of celebration, ceremony, or well-earned recreation
continue to give rise to the unending anthology of American folk
music.

What an array of regions—country and urban—and of moods—
witty, poetic, realistic, cynical, raunchy, reverent—and of talents

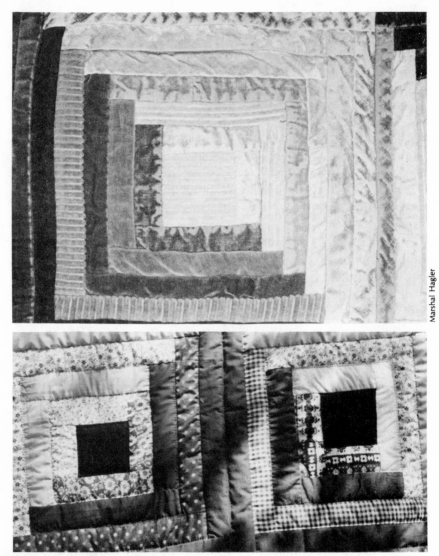

Marshal Hagler

Variety in Unity: Two quilts, separated by time (one is antique; the other is recent) and space (one is from the Ozarks; the other is from the Kentucky hills). The geometric "Log Cabin" pattern is the same in each. Yet infinite variations are possible as a result of differences in colors chosen, their sequence, and the frequency of their repetition. Moreover, variations in combining dark and light pieces or solids and prints give every quilt in this traditional pattern a unique life of its own.

are involved in the blues alone. Here is infinite variety in unity. The blues, like most quilts, too, are constructed from a limited set of patterns or formulas. Yet the bluesman is a virtuoso. He collects songs; he composes new ones in the traditional style, which also makes him something of a poet; he improvises on set pieces; he arranges his music; he sings as well and often plays several

At the Ozark Folk Center, Mountain View, Arkansas, Lois Dodson at her quilting frame is putting design stitches into a traditional "Double Wedding Ring" quilt.

instruments. The contents of his lyrics reveal him to be something of a social analyst, and his showmanship in performance is pure artistry.

The woman who quilts is no less talented and no more self-conscious of her many and varied skills than is the bluesman. In her visual and textured rather than aural and verbal medium, she too is a virtuoso in collecting, arranging, improvising, and composing. And her art also—in one of America's least interrupted and most widespread traditions—seems to generate social analysis or philosophy.

From Marie D. Webster's 1915 publication, *Quilts, Their Story and How to Make Them*, we get this record of one Kentucky woman's insight:

"How much piecin' a quilt is like livin' a life! Many a time I've set and listened to Parson Page preachin' about predestination and free will, and I've said to myself, 'If I could just git up in the pulpit with one of my quilts I could make it a heap plainer to folks than parson's makin' it with his big words.' You see, you start out with jest so much caliker; you don't go to the store and pick it out and buy it, but the neighbors will give you a piece here and a piece there, and you'll have a piece left over every time you cut a dress, and you take jest what happens to come. And that's like predestination. But when it comes to the cuttin' out, why, you're free to choose your own pattern. You can give the same kind o' pieces to two persons, and one'll make a 'Nine Patch' and one'll make a 'Wild-Goose Chase,' and there'll be two quilts made out of the same kind of pieces, and jest as different as they can be. And that is jest the way with livin'. The Lord sends us the pieces, but we can cut them out and put 'em together pretty much to suit ourselves, and there's a heap more in the cuttin' out and the sewin' than there is in the caliker."

The bluesman might talk about the freedom to choose his own forms (twelve-bar, sixteen-bar, eight-bar) and tunings (open, E and A, or C, G, D), letting "melody lines" replace "caliker," for the truth in the Kentucky quilter's observations applies universally.

Equipped with avid interest, tape recorder, camera, and note pad, seek out either one of these artists. She may live quietly in private, a widow, perhaps, who stitches her bereavement and her legacy into gifts for her grandchildren; or she may, sociably, like to chat and quilt for the needy at a frame set up for ten or more women at someone's home or at a center for "seniors."

He will be right in the center of an extended family of enthusiasts, whether you have to ask around to find him in a Southern hamlet so small some maps exclude it or find him in the phone directory of a medium-sized town, only to learn that he's on tour in Poland and won't be back till next month; you might even find him in an out-of-the-way tavern not listed in the yellow pages of that city's directory. There are other places to look. Nor is the musician always a man nor the quilter always a woman. But in these two forms of folk art alone is plenty enough for a lifetime of fascinated appreciation.

Collect from the folklore that is all around you. You may not have to look any farther than across the street, as demonstrated in this

Marshal Hagler

Broadax—hand forged and crafted by David Matthews, Ozark Folk Center, Mountain View, Arkansas.

segment of recorded dialogue between dulcimer maker Reagan Cole and this collector:

Cole: *A man I know in Eureka, he owns a house across the street. I guess he's just getting real close to eighty. And he's got wonderful stories to tell, and he loves to talk.*
Interviewer: The message in my book is that if there's a person like that living across the street from you, go over there with your tape recorder; or at least listen good, make some notes, and write them up when you get back home.
Cole: *I'm going to try to get him to show me how to cut out a railroad tie with a broadax.*
Interviewer: I hope you don't pass up that opportunity. Early Americans could do almost anything with a broadax. Go back over there. Bring your camera and your cassette recorder. He'll be so proud to show you. And you'll have the time of your life recording it all, plus an invaluable folklore collector's item.

Harvesting Grass Roots: In Your Own Backyard

Be Your Own Folklore Resource

You can be your own best informant. For a rewarding initial experience as a collector of folklore, sit down with yourself and conduct an "intra-view."

But first have a smooth-flowing pen, a short stack of 8½" x 11" (standard size) note sheets, and a generous stack of 4" x 6" cards. (The 5" x 8" size is unwieldy while 3" x 5" cards are often too small.) Now pour yourself a cup of coffee or tea, a glass of milk or beer. But do get comfortable. You are going to mine your memory to discover a rich source of folklore.

There aren't many hermits, and you'd have to be a hermit not to be in several shared interest groups. So, for openers make an inventory of the folk groups to which you belong by reason of your ethnic heritage, your occupation, where you live, your age, your religious affiliation, your hobbies, your sports activities, any interest that consistently brings interaction with a group of folks.

Now you can dig for the folklore embedded in your memory by asking yourself questions like these: What are some of the sayings, the inside traditions and lingo, the gags and customs that bind us together as a folk group? (Special lingo or informal terminology is always a dead giveaway.) What humorous anecdotes (true or not) circulate about us?

Center brief responses on 4" x 6" cards, one to a card. Write detailed narratives on 8½" x 11" sheets, one to a sheet (and all on one sheet, if possible). Continue these questions, which are based on folk group situations, responding as motivated. However, you've barely started.

How did some of the terminology that circulates only in our family and nobody else's come about? Was it children's natural creativity, for instance, or did we all adopt one of the children's mispronunciations and turn it into a word we've all used for years? (Include such situational data below the entry.)

What are some of the nicknames we use with each other that nobody else knows about? What about the same sort of thing in my family when I was a child? Did we have a family whistle? (You could always record that on tape and discuss it on a card.) Did we have special names for certain dishes my mother used to prepare? Did my dad have particular sayings that I still associate with him? Did we have traditional ways of celebrating birthdays or even secular holidays (like Halloween) that none of the other families had? Did I import any of these family traditions into my own family once I grew up?

What are some of the fun rhymes, game songs, riddle jokes, tongue twisters, or limericks I used to say as a kid? What are some of the remedies my Aunt Edna used to practice on us kids when we took ill? What are some of the teas my mother used to brew herself to help us get over a sickness?

What were some of those word games and number tricks we once entertained ourselves with in study hall? Do I know any counting-out rhymes from preschool? spelling rhymes from grade school? mock athletic cheers from high school? military cadence chants from the service? (If they were OK to sing then, there's no justification for censorship in your collection.)

What were my retorts when another kid insulted me at school? What's my favorite wisecrack or "slam saying" now? What's the funniest line of graffiti I've ever read from a wall or desk top? Where was it and how long ago? What little superstition do I permit myself when I'm especially uptight and sure could use some luck? or when I'm trying to help matters along just a little so the fish'll bite? or maybe at New Year's time? (Record these on 4" x 6" cards.)

What's my favorite joke of all time? (Use an 8½" x 11" sheet to record narrative jokes; they're folktales.) What are the outlandish lyrics to well-known songs my kids bring home from school? While you're at it, if there are any kids in your home, you might want to ask them directly, "How do you entertain yourselves in study hall?"

Verbal Lore

Now that you're getting the hang of it, take a different track to the same destination. Here are some questions organized by types of short verbal folklore. Respond to as many as you can by saying to yourself, "No, but I've heard someone say . . . ."

Folk lingo: Have you ever heard a young driver say, "I think I'll go *crank* up the car?" In your geographical area, does anyone ever *carry* you to the party when promising you a ride? Have you ever heard folks in the southern part of North Carolina call baby chicks *peepies* or *dibs?* When a person wears pants so short they'd be good for wading home in a downpour, have you heard them teasingly called *floods* or *high water britches?* Have you ever heard a golfer refer to a low ball as a *worm burner,* or a parachutist talk about *honking on the toggles,* or a host ask you to *B.Y.O.B.,* or a musician say, "Where'd I leave my *ax?*"

Proverbial folksay: Has anyone ever described your next meal as "po'k, rolls, and grits"? ("We'll poke our feet under the table, roll our eyes, and grit our teeth," as one Southern dad likes to say.) How about these true proverbs? "Improvement begins with I." "Youth is a gift of nature; age is a work of art." "No matter how high and mighty you get, the size of your funeral will still depend on the weather." "If today were a fish, I'd throw it back." "Just because I've ordered doesn't mean I have to stop looking at the menu."

When you ask folks the same old "how are you?", do you ever get "same old six and seven," or " 'bout like common," instead of "fine"? How do folks describe indeterminate distances? Ever hear "about a mile an' a bit"? Ever know someone so persuasive she could talk a stump into moving six feet? Was anything ever so good you couldn't beat that with a stick? so good it made you want to slap your mama? as plain as the nose on your face? as high as a Georgia

pine? finer than frog's hair and not near as scarce? full as a tick? so
good you could eat it with one foot in the fire? as ugly as homemade
sin? so old it came off Noah's ark?

Were you ever told, "Do that again and I'll cloud up and rain on
you"? "If you had a brain, you'd be dangerous"? And did you reply,
"*Boss* spelled backwards is double-s-o-b"? or "When they passed
out brains, you thought they said *trains* and said, 'I'll wait for the
next one' "? or "Why don't you make like a tree and leave"? or
"Make like a banana and split"?

Have you ever known anyone "two bricks shy of a load"? When
you say the same thing at the same time as the person you're with,
do you both interlock pinkies while one says, "Pins," and the other
says, "Needles"? Bet you could fill in the remaining dialogue that
precedes making a wish.

Did you ever trade "authors and titles" with friends, like "*Dash to
the Outhouse* by Willie Makit, illustrated by Betty Dont"? or "*Over
the Cliff* by Hugo First, illustrated by Aileen Dover"? Do you know
any other Wellerisms besides " 'I see,' said the blind man as he
picked up his hammer and saw"? Do you know any more palindromes like "able was I ere I saw Elba"? (Read it backwards.) How's
your collection of "Confucius say"? or Tom Swifties (e.g., "'Let's go
to the stable,' said Tom hoarsely")?

Riddling lore: "Brothers and sisters have I none, but this boy's father
is my father's son." (The implied question is "Who am I?") Do you
know what they call little white dogs in Alaska? (puppies.) Those
were riddling questions—the kind you can figure out the answer to,
if you're clever enough to weed out the surplus information
contained in the question.

Bet you can't answer these, though: What happens if you cross a
canary with a blender?" (shredded tweet.) "What's purple and goes
'slam, slam, slam, slam'?" (a four-door grape.) The reason you can't
solve them unless you've heard them before is that they're riddle
jokes—told for the fun the teller can have revealing the play-on-
words answers to you.

How many "knock-knock" dialogues can you come up with? Do
you know any "over and under" sentences? Here's one:

stand	take	to	world
I	you	throw	the

Read over and under until you get *I* under *stand, you* under *take, to* over *throw,* and *the* under *world:* "I understand you undertake to overthrow the underworld!"

Know any pretended obscene riddles, the kind that aren't obscene at all, except in the associative mind of the listener? Here's an example: "What does a man do on two legs, that a dog does on three legs, that a woman does sitting down?" Answer: shake hands. The reverse can happen with tongue twisters. Did anyone ever ask you to repeat a perfectly innocent-sounding tongue twister—until you found yourself very embarrassed by what you said when your tongue got twisted? Well, you can try this one out in public; it's safe—very difficult, though. "Six slick slim sycamore saplings."

Folk rhymes: Can you supply the final lines to these: "One potato, two potato, three potato, four . . . "? "Eenie, meenie, mynie, mo . . . "? Did you used to say, "If he hollers let him go" or "If he hollers make him pay"? And did you add the tag "out you go, you old dirty dishrag, you" and also, "My mama taught me to pick this one"? What other counting-out rhymes do you remember? Know any jump rope rhymes? How many ways can you finish "Cinderella, dressed in yella . . . "? or "Down in the meadow where the green grass grows . . . "? Here's a whole one that comes from Dallas, Texas. You have to be good to make it to ten with your eyes closed:

> Blondie and Dagwood went downtown
> Blondie wore an evening gown
> Dagwood wore a pair of shoes
> Cookie read the evening news
> And this is what it said:
> Close your eyes and count to ten
> If you miss, you'll take an end.

Kind of takes you back, doesn't it?
How about spelling rhymes?

> *M, i,* crooked letter, crooked letter,
> *i,* crooked letter, crooked letter, *i,*
> hump back, hump back, *i*

That spelling rhyme (for *Mississippi*) isn't really a rhyme at all, but you have to admit it's in verse. Not all folk rhymes actually rhyme, but these last three do. You should be able to come up with at least three of your own for each. The first two are limericks. (It's not easy to collect G-rated ones; most are X-rated, which need not in the least deter you from collecting them.)

> A flea and a fly in a flu
> Were imprisoned, so what could they do?
> Said the flea, "Let us fly."
> Said the fly, "Let us flee."
> So they fled through a flaw in a flu.

> There once was a man named Dwight,
> Whose speed was much faster than light.
> He set out one day
> In a relative way,
> And returned on the previous night.

The third example is a belief rhyme—like a superstition, only in verse:

> See a pin and pick it up,
> All the day, you'll have good luck.
> See a pin and let it lie,
> You'll be sorry by and by.

Folk beliefs: How many hiccough cures can you remember? Are they as effective as "go behind a door and don't think of a fox"? or "kiss a red-haired boy"? Did you know that lots of folks think it's bad luck to say "thank you" to someone who gives you a plant as a gift? You may say, "That's a lovely plant" or "I'm going to enjoy watching this grow," but not "Thank you."

What's it supposed to mean if your palm itches, nose itches, ear rings, second toe is longer than the others? Do you know what one *has* to say after experiencing a quick chill? "A rabbit ran over my grave." And have you heard that for good luck, on the first day of every month your first word should be "rabbit"? or that dreaming of a death harbingers a wedding? Can you get someone to tell you why you'll never see a bluejay on Friday? Has anyone ever told you that feathers in the pillow of a good person's death bed will plait themselves into a crown?

Heightened Awareness: Serving as your own best informant heightens awareness. You'll soon begin to notice how abundantly short forms of verbal lore, in particular, seem to crop up wherever you go. You'll notice the interesting turns of phrase (dialect vocabulary) that habitually liven the speech patterns of someone you know in Atlanta, who hails from Port Arthur, Texas, or the never-ending supply of elephant riddle jokes, virtually a customer service, provided by the owner of a downtown shoe store that caters to school children: "Why do elephants sit on marshmallows? To keep their feet out of the hot chocolate!" "How do you stop an elephant from charging?" "Take away his credit card!"

You'll recognize certain gestures and utterances of a bridge partner or poker buddy as traditional gamblers' superstitions. You'll overhear folk cures in the supermarket: "Toothpaste on mosquito bites kills the itching"; proverbial phrases in elevators: "What I know about science, you can put in a flea's navel, and still have enough room for two caraway seeds and an ant's heart!"; and parody rhymes from your children: "I'm Popeye, the sailor man, / I live in a garbage can. / I eat all the worms / and spit out the germs. / I'm Popeye, the sailor man." or "Humpty-Dumpty sat on the wall. / Humpty-Dumpty had a great fall. / All the king's horses and all the king's men / Had scrambled eggs."

You'll take down witty graffiti in restrooms: "Visit San Clemente, you paid for it"; dialect pronunciations in neighborhood shopping malls, "Warshin' this new dress just 'rurned' it!"

Collecting Folklore Effectively

If your own recollections of traditional lore are surfacing fast and furiously, just keep on jotting them down until you run out of steam. Then you can go back and complete each card or sheet by adding appropriate subject headings, the situational data, and the collector-informant identifications.

In the South, the first query exchanged by folks just getting acquainted is "where are you from?" In one way or another we are all bound up in our sense of place— one region or a combination of regions (for Americans are characterized by mobility) where we grew up and where our ancestors lived. But the network of our cultural identity (where we come from) also includes rank in the family and community—order of birth (place in the family) and occupational and social place.

Whether recording a peculiar turn of phrase (an example of regional folk dialect) or the entire process of shingle making from the felling of the tree to the construction of the roof, the folklore collector must view the maker and the artifact as extensions of situation, carefully noting the answers to "where are you from?" down to the informant's present address (and, if necessary, the instructions for finding it).

Experience helps us develop the knack for asking sufficient questions, for knowing when to remain silent, for making informants feel comfortable in our presence. But even before setting out to acquire such experience, the collector-to-be needs to know that a folklore collection is authentic, thus valuable, only insofar as each item is placed—identified in its context.

The following illustrations provide general guidelines and exemplify, in specific, two of the most commonly experienced collecting situations: verbal folklore overheard in public and the verbal item obtained while interacting with an informant known to the collector.

Here then are the categories of information which make a folkloric item truly collectible.

FRONT OF CARD

Type and subtype(s) of folklore   (Optional)
(See Appendix A)   Classification
                                    Code Number
                                    (See Appendix A)

The Item Collected. Place in quotation marks if it is rendered word for word as heard. Omit quotation marks if the item is being quoted indirectly.

Give any explanatory comments or illustrative examples which would clarify this item for someone who might never have heard it before.

BACK OF CARD

Your name or initials, as collector
The date (of writing this card)

Your informant's name (who may be yourself) and/or gender; regional location (county, city, state); age (exact or approximate); ethnicity (if remotely relevant).

Context: Where and when informant recalls hearing this item for the first time, how long ago that was, anything else about the informant's situation that might shed light on the function or purpose of this item.

(Of course, you can only make this side of the card as specific as circumstances allow. But without such "documentation" collected items would have no archival value.)

A collection card, all made out, would look something like this:

FRONT

Folk dialect—Nickname—Food   I.D.4.C.

"Hoover Hogs"

What Ray and Paula Stevens, my maternal grandparents, used to call
the rabbits they were able to trap and cook during the Depression
years. They considered themselves fortunate to get them.

E.g., "What's for dinner tonight, Mom?"
      "Hoover hogs, son."

BACK

JRB
6/18/78

I remember Mom telling me this, for the first time, about fifteen years
ago.   We were living in Chattanooga at the time.   But Gram and
Gramps were eating these rabbits during the thirties while they lived
in Fredericksburg, Virginia.

Here's how a short form collection card might look if you entered
an overheard item without obtaining informant-data as specific as

that which you can obtain from yourself or from anyone with whom you have a chance to talk:

FRONT

Folk dialect—Word form   I.A.

"Careful, or you'll *tump* it over!"

Tump seems to mean "knock over or capsize."

2036246

BACK

S.D.
3/6/72
Columbus, Mississippi

   Heard a young black mother say that to her child in a dept. store. He'd set a lg. soft drink down on the floor close to his mother who was shopping at a counter.

P.S. 7/10/72 Heard a white fella in his twenties use the same expression.

Classifying verbal lore: Because you want to have fun reading through whatever parts of your collection interest you at any given moment, you should follow some sort of consistent filing system. Nothing terribly complicated, you understand, but one that enables you efficiently to put away likes with likes and later to retrieve any categories and subcategories of lore, including variation. Whatever the system you decide to adopt or devise, you should label the cards and sheets in your collection as you go so that you'll never get bogged down in the mechanics rather than the fun of collecting.

The procedure for classifying and arranging material in a short form collection is essentially the same as for longer forms. A convenient, informal classification outline has been placed in the Appendix at the end of this book and is devised to serve just such a growing collection as yours. Since it can be applied in as great or small a degree of particularity as a collector finds appropriate, it should prove adequate to your needs. Moreover, you can use it as is, modify it as you wish, or improvise your own system.

Folklore Begets Folklore

Verbal folklore is for harvesting actively as well as for over-hearing. Your short forms collection is likely to be more voluminous, on the one hand, if only because long forms cannot usually be written out as quickly as one hears them. On the other hand, the long forms require more space than an index card allows. Besides, anecdotal reminiscences, tales, legends, games, and pastimes will crop up in abundance on taped interviews.

Just as folklore takes on many shapes, harvesting it can involve several activities—sociable conversation, direct information gathering, picture taking, and sound recording—in addition to making written records. But whatever the format for recording remembered beliefs, narratives, songs and sayings, bear in mind that it takes one from the collector for the informant to know one.

The more familiar you become with the content of your own collection, the more effective your efforts will be at prompting the retrieval of such lore from the memories of others. Folklore begets folklore.

Getting Others to Share Their Lore

Folk remedies: Avoid asking your friends general questions about folk cures, folktales, legends, and folk songs. Ask your friends specific questions. What have they heard will get rid of warts? You'll reap a bonus. What do they do for poison ivy? Rub on vinegar and rhubarb juice? How did they relieve coughs prior to "nighttime cold medicine," as they say on TV? You'll get variants galore on taking doses of turpentine with whiskey, lemon, and honey, sorghum, or sugar. Esoteric examples trigger esoteric memories. Did they ever hear of a boiled peach leaves poultice for a sprain? How practical is the belief that a lemon rind will draw a deeply embedded splinter to the surface?

Folktales: Share a tale; get several in return. Folktales, the narrative fiction of the folk—pure entertainment, always amusing, occasionally moralistic, not necessarily humorous—usually occur in appropriately sociable contexts, more often than not from the lips of habitual story- or joketellers. But if you want to create a situation conducive to storytelling, build your own repertory. Tales can be as old as the fable of the fox and the sour grapes or as modern as traveling salesman jokes or "shaggy dog" stories.

The latter have very little to do with dogs, but you will recognize the type from this variant of a widely circulated tale collected verbatim from Ross Gray in New Orleans:

Once there was a man, an animal trainer, who decided that he would go to the beach and capture several aquatic animals, porpoises in this case. He took them to his residence and gave them a magic elixir whereby they became immortal—ever-living. Because the trainer could see how homesick the porpoises were, he returned to the beach to collect some driftwood, sand, larkspur, and even some young sea gulls for them, so that they should not miss their original surroundings so much.

While bringing back all this paraphernalia and the gulls, he chanced upon a traffic jam on the highway near his house. Unbeknownst to him, a circus train had had an accident, and a very old, senile lion had escaped and was reposing in the bushes near the man's house. He left his car with his arms full of sea gulls and started up the hill to his home. On his way, he tripped over the lion in the bushes.

A nearby policeman saw what happened and ran over to arrest the man at once. He demanded to know the charges, which were: transporting young gulls across a staid lion for immortal porpoises.

As you can see, the shaggy dog tale is a plethora of far-fetched material threaded together with the thinnest logic, because the whole thing is just an excuse for an outrageous extended pun at the end.

Beliefs and belief tales: Bringing up an interesting superstition is like casting bread upon the waters, and perhaps also the converse when it comes to the belief collected from an elderly black informant, who insists that spitting on a piece of bread and feeding it to one's dog will keep the pet from straying. Do not be put off by the syndrome of denial when the subject is superstition. Talk about "beliefs" instead if you will, but as soon as folks assure you they're not superstitious, listen for the *but* which follows.

Mary Harper's recollection of folkways in the Appalachian foothills is demonstrative:

On Sand Mountain, where I grew up, we were taught to be ashamed if we were superstitious. And we weren't superstitious, unless it was about a hoot owl hootin' in the yard at night. That was a sign of death. I know it used to make me feel bad; I didn't know who was going to die next.

Belief tales, or legends, the long-form counterparts of superstitions, are less subject to face-saving denials and more prone to affirmation by hearsay. Someone might tell you a ghost story (supernatural legend about a revenant) with the qualification, "I know this can't be true, but my cousin heard it from her neighbor who swears it really happened to her."

If you want to solicit legendry actively, you first need to be your own informant again, so that you can collect by donating. Take stock of the belief tales you already know that are associated with sites, characters, heroes, historical periods, sensational or supernatural events—told in your family, locally, regionally, or in your occupation.

Perhaps you already know some religious legends. Explanatory tales with reference to Biblical elements (though the Bible is not their true source) are known as the "Bible of the folk." One example of this narrative type accounts for the shape and coloration of the dogwood flower on the grounds that the Cross of Jesus was made of a dogwood tree.

You are likely to be familiar with examples of a highly prevalent type of modern legendry known as the "urban belief tale" (because it features elements of urban technology). Rarely associated with legendry, urban belief tales may find their way into newspaper reports despite their supernatural or bizarre plots. One widespread version of this type concerns a phantom hitchhiker:

A driver picks up a young woman who is hitchhiking home. She gets in the backseat and converses with the driver, who maintains eye contact by means of his rearview mirror. When she tells him she feels chilly, he hands back his sweater for her to wear. Driving her all the way to the home address she has given him, he gets out of the car to open her door, only to find her gone. Puzzled, he walks to the door of her residence. His ring is answered by an elderly woman, who tells him she frequently receives inquiries similar to his. The only young girl who ever lived at this address is her daughter, who does indeed answer to the driver's description, but who died many years ago. She mentions the girl's name and where she is buried. Too puzzled to simply continue his journey, the driver goes to the cemetery and locates the girl's tombstone, where, neatly folded, lies his sweater.

Folk songs: The category of folk songs is broader than what you might expect if you associate it primarily with the material on commercially recorded albums by well-known folk singers. Actually, folk songs are all those songs we pick up informally (without the aid of formal instruction or printed music) from early childhood on. You've heard them at home, at school on the playground, at camp, in church groups, on picnics; and you've sung them, and still do, with your family or your friends.

Kids are treasuries of parody songs. For children love to poke fun at whatever their elders take most seriously, like death: "The worms crawl in, the worms crawl out . . . ." Remember that one? And, certainly, romantic love. One popular song which spent many months atop the bygone "hit parade" began:

> *You smile, the song begins,*
> *You speak, and I hear violins;*
> *It's magic.*

The parody may have outlasted the original. For years, youngsters have destroyed romantic moments for love-struck older brothers and sisters, serenading them inopportunely:

> *You smile, your teeth fall out;*
> *Your hair, it smells like sauerkraut;*
> *It's tragic.*

Folk songs can be functional, like work songs or lullabies; they can be lyrical—by far the largest group— or they can be narrative. They can be religious or secular, serious or humorous, packed with meaning or pure nonsense. They vary more, live longer, and appeal to a wider diversity of people than any other types of songs in the world.

When you collect them on the tape recorder, you have the words and music to entertain you. But you can also collect lyrics and their variants by setting them down on paper, thus enjoying them as oral literature in the same way as other forms of collected verbal lore.

You can sit down with yourself and retrieve a good portion of your own repertory by remembering family and other group occasions on which informal singing took place fairly regularly. Note whether the situations were family rituals (like bedtime or meals), social events, trips, or celebrations. You can ask folks old or young to recall their own favorite lullabies or fun songs as well as songs (whatever the type) learned from their mothers. Or, to collect songs, you can place yourself in a situation that you know will produce them—a school children's excursion, for example.

Riding the bus with your school-age children or grandchildren, as an adult chaperone on a field trip, you could come home with an anthology of children's folk songs:

> *Ninety-nine bottles of beer on the wall,*
> *Ninety-nine bottles of beer,*
> *If one of those bottles should happen to fall,*
> *Ninety-eight bottles of beer on the wall.*
>
> *Ninety-eight bottles of beer on the wall,*
> *Ninety-eight bottles of beer, . . .*

and so on, interminably, until all ninety-nine bottles have fallen or, in variation, have been taken down and turned around.

A much-loved parody to the tune of "The Battle Hymn of the Republic" draws familiar chuckles from understanding teachers:

> *Glory, glory, hallelujah!*
> *Teacher hit me with a ruler.*
> *I met her at the door*
> *With a loaded forty-four,*
> *And she ain't my teacher any more.*

No group bus trip would be complete without it and at least one parody on a true folk song:

> *On top of Old Smokie,*
> *All covered with sand,*
> *I shot my poor teacher,*
> *With a red rubber band.*
>
> *I shot her with pleasure,*
> *I shot her with pride.*
> *How could I have missed her?*
> *She's forty foot wide.*

> *I went to her funeral.*
> *I went to her grave.*
> *Some people threw flowers,*
> *I threw a grenade.*

In the very next breath, however, those noisy, irreverent icono-clasts in tee shirts may turn the bus scene into a revival meeting with this angelic rendition:

(Chorus)
Rise and shine and give God the glory-glory,
Rise and shine and give God the glory-glory,
Rise and shine and (clap) give God the glory-glory,
Children of the Lord.

Pastimes: Like folk songs and superstitions, pastimes are really only partly verbal. Folk songs have music; superstitions as well as songs and games are often attended by gestures and props. Props are necessary in pastimes like handed-down card tricks or desktop football, which involves paper folded according to prescribed rules. With a little prompting, most folks can remember practical jokes, like phoning the drugstore to inquire if they have Prince Albert in a can, then shouting to the poor clerk who says, "Yes," "Well, why don't you let him out!" before slamming down the receiver to peals of childish laughter.

What kinds of competitive "spotting" games are you familiar with from long automobile trips? Do they involve landmarks, animals, or license plates? The following game, already traditional when Mary Harper would play it with several brothers and sisters, is one of virtually thousands of variant guessing games:

We used to play "Pretty Bird in My Cup. What Sort's Yours?" It was a guessing game. We knew the names of lots of birds, some of 'em we never had seen, that probably never had been in America, probably from the English birds. But we had a long string of "pretty-birds-in-my-cup-what-sort's-yours." We had to give them the letter that they started off with, and if none of them could still guess it, we'd maybe give them three letters. That's about as far as we would go.

We [the guessers] had a wet rag. And when we'd guess the name, we'd throw it in their faces. Then the one that guessed it had to get up and play "Pretty Bird," and that would be the one who put the questions to us.

Occupational Lore

From coal miners to flight attendants, all occupational groups share folk traditions often manifesting a generic gamut of verbal lore. College students, for instance, are an occupational group. There is folklore in academe, elite though the environment may be.

You know that "Do you know any campus lore?" is bound to be ineffectual. Start the ball rolling with something like "How long do you usually wait for a professor who doesn't show up in class on time?" You'll get an immediate answer. Ask several students separately. You'll get so many variations you'll know you've struck folklore. Most students sincerely believe that the informal custom of giving a teacher just so long to arrive at the lectern before they vacate the lecture hall is a rule of the college.

Ask a collegiate friend if there are any traditional beliefs associated with campus statuary or monuments. One tongue-in-cheek belief widely circulated in academe is that a brick will drop from a monument or statue topple from its pedestal in the event that a virgin should happen to pass by. Ask for stories about professors reputed to be "characters." What are some of the outlandish things attributed to their speech or behavior in the classroom? These are likely subjects of campus legends.

Ask whether any buildings on campus are said to be haunted. Students may know of several, ranging from dormitories to historic landmarks. Ask if any sorority or fraternity house is rumored to have a body bricked up in its walls. Collect rites of passage by inquiring about what takes place when a fraternity man announces to his brothers that he's just pinned a girl?

Here are two examples of occupational legendry as you might record them on sheets of paper for your own collection:

LEGEND: Local-Historical-Occupational/VI.D.11.12
Birmingham steel mills
(Front side only)

   "Mr. D_____ said that it was so bad in Birmingham (Alabama)
around the steel mills (at the turn of the century) that somebody could
walk in to apply for a job, and they'd say, 'Well, I'm sorry sir, we don't
have an opening right now, but if you'll just sit down over there in a
few minutes somebody will get killed, and you can take his place!'"

   Collected by E.S.K. from Mr. Luther Brooks, Nashville, Tennessee,
March 16, 1978. Brooks is forty. Lived in Nashville all his life.
   We were talking at length about the legend of Hazel Farris (See tape
3-16-78) when D_____'s name came up and Brooks remembered
what the former had said about Birmingham. D_____ retired to
Nashville from Birmingham. He and Brooks knew one another some
twenty years ago. Mr. Brooks wanted to be sure that I knew he didn't
have anything critical to say about today's Birmingham.

(Although this entry is short enough to be on a 4" x 6" card, most
legendary lore takes up more space. You wouldn't want some
legends on cards and some on sheets. That would create filing
problems.)

LEGEND: Local-Occupational/VI.D.12
Birmingham steel mills–railroading
(Front)
The One That Got Away (collector's title)

   "I shouldn't even tell anybody that, but about five years ago, no,
seven years ago, they really went remote and cut the engineers and
firemen off. Five men used to work a train—one engine: one engineer,
the firemens, a conductor, and two switchmen. Well, they cut all
them folks off, and they made an operator and a helper out of
them—what they wanted to continue. And that's the way we
worked—two men.

   "But, right after they first went remote, they just put 'em on our
smallest engines to start with to see if they really worked—63 and 64
was the smallest engines they had. And one of the guys, he'd gotten
real fancy with it, and he was making it work. Everybody else was
making it not work, so he was the only one making it work. So they

sent him around to the back side of the tin mill and switched one of the tracks. And they just had three cars on the side of the engine. They had three to set out and three to set back in.

"Anyway, he switched some scrap out and got back on. And he was on the north end of his train. And he had a couple of cars ahead of him, the engine in the middle of it, and three cars behind it. He started rolling, and he thought he had it going. But whenever he'd get back, the next thing you know, he'd stop. Well, after he went down the track a little ways, he'd just stop. He looked around him, and he didn't have any engine!

"It had gone the *other* way! Went through to the end of the track, in through a big old tin building, right on through the restroom where guys was sittin'. [Everybody breaks up laughing.] They said it took about a half dozen rolls of toilet paper to get them boys out!

"It was amazing. I mean, it went through a—went through a big old tin building too. Never hurt anything. Didn't hurt nobody. We never killed nobody. (The laughter has yet to subside.) Yeah. Just sittin' there with his britches down, watching that thing, that engine comin' on."

From Ann, another listener: "Like, 'Oh Lordy, this is the way I'm gonna go!'"

(The quotation marks signify that this is a word-for-word rendition. When the collector records an item indirectly—that is, in his or her own words, after hearing it from an informant, quotation marks are omitted.)

(Back)

Collected by E.S.K. on two occasions, because I wanted to verify some details. March 10 and March 24, 1978. March 10 account is given here.

Informant: Lendal McCullar, in his forties, from Gardendale, Alabama.

Situations: Each time, I was interviewing a group about the subject of clog dancing. See tapes 3/10/78 and 3/24-25/78. Before I began, I asked Lendal about his occupation. The following comes from the second tape. We are at a long table in a Tuscaloosa restaurant.

Context: Lendal tells me that he runs a railroad engine for U. S. Steel in Birmingham. "I run an engine by remote control." Ann Blizzard and I are both eager to learn just how remote, remote engineering really is. This is the dialogue leading up to the story:

Lendal: "I'm sittin' outside the engine, on the train. I go inside and turn my switches on, and put on a pack, and put on a belt with the controls strapped onto my stomach. And I work my switches and get everything turned to where it will be remote. And I walk out and don't go back in the engine anymore. We're on the train somewhere. Now, I can run it five thousand yards away from me, if I need to, if I think it's safe and can see that distance. I'm doing five men's jobs—everything. And right today, I'm not getting paid what I was gettin' in 1972."

Ann: "Suppose you have a problem—if they have one man on that train who can run it, and you have a problem?"

Lendal: "If I fall down or if anything happens to me, my engine automatically goes into 'emergency.' My pack on my back, it's got a 'dead man's switch' in it, and if I stay bent over so many seconds, my engine will go into emergency and put the brakes on, and the system won't operate." I ask Lendal to repeat the story he told me March 10. Ann's husband, Bill Blizzard, who works for a railroad ("the one Casey Jones used to work for, and Jimmie Rogers, you know") and was fresh out of legends himself, had fortuitously asked Lendal, "Have you ever lost a train?"

See if you can get a lawyer to tell you some jokes about doctors, and vice versa. (Members of these occupations are traditional rivals.) Collect computer programmers' jokes. Ask a hairdresser or barber about a grizzly story (urban belief tale) concerning the fate of a woman who kept her beehive hairdo laquered in place for months without combing it out. If your contact doesn't know that one, you'll probably end up with another tale just as good.

Inquire of doctors or nurses about remedies or beliefs heard from patients concerning the human body; ask an obstetrician about traditional beliefs concerning pregnancy. If you're a woman, note instances of ribaldry among women only; if you're a man, locker room humor is collectible.

Whether you collect at random, by the "vacuum cleaner method," or become more narrowly interested, say, in superstitions and proverbs, remember two guiding principles: First, familiarity with your own collection breeds content. Be able to share a priest-minister-rabbi joke with your clergyman to hear three more, a planting belief with a gardener to reap several others.

And, finally, though an informant might insist that your way of telling an item is "wrong" and give it back to you the "right way" (translate "familiar"), there are no right or wrong texts in oral circulation, only variants. Don't pass up an item just because you think you've heard it before. Say, "Tell it," not "Yes," if someone wants to know whether you've already heard the one about . . . .

From a couple of youngsters you might collect this circular proverbial dialogue, to discover when you bring it home to file that an older informant once gave you a version in which the magazine costs a dime and the second speaker only has a nickel:

> 1st: *That's life!*
> 2nd: *What's life?*
> 1st: Life *is a magazine.*
> 2nd: *How much does it cost?*
> 1st: *Fifty cents.*
> 2nd: *But I've only got a quarter.*
> 1st: *That's life.*
> 2nd: *What's life?* . . . .

The more varied your collection, the more it will reveal to you about life and people being most themselves.

Tools of the Folklore Trade

S o far, you have been writing down mostly shorter forms of folklore gathered from yourself, your friends, and from casual conversations. But folklore takes many shapes, and there are other ways for the collector to record and document them. Involved are audio-visual tools and your person-to-person interaction with folks who are the main resources of the verbal and material folk culture that interests you. As with any vocation or avocation, familiarity with the necessary tools is a prerequisite to the enjoyment that interviewing brings.

Ideally, you need something to write on, a means for recording sound, and something to take pictures with. In these and other respects a great many options are open to you. The rule of thumb used in this book is "maximum simplicity for optimal effectiveness." Don't spend more money on equipment than you absolutely need to. Use what works best. But don't ever stint on the amounts of paper, audio tape, or film necessary to the success of a project.

Whether your tools of the trade are a notebook from the dime store or an engraved volume from an exclusive boutique, it's the notes that will count. Whether you carry an expensive camera and complicated accessories, a small pocket Instamatic, or a sketchbook, it's pictorial accuracy that is your primary concern. The same goes for aural accuracy and your recording equipment. Stereophonic recordings of folk music do it best justice, of course, but unless you find it acceptable to pay for and transport several pounds of bulky equipment, you're better off with a reliable portable cassette machine.

Stationery Supplies

Single-handedly, when it comes to using 4" x 6" index cards, the active collector can practically cause a rise in the market. Index cards are indispensable for documenting short forms of verbal folklore. One's short-form collection can be arranged in shoe or file boxes most conveniently if: (a) all the cards in a collection are the same size, and (b) if the practice of making each item self-contained is consistently followed.

It is terribly important that you develop the card-carrying habit. As an amateur collector, you never want to leave home without a few 4" x 6" cards stashed somewhere on your person.

The Recorder and Recording

The interviews conducted for this book were recorded on a lightweight, compact tape machine which cost under $100. Not much bigger than a 4" x 6" index card, such a recorder is easy to transport and to handhold during interviews when no convenient furniture is present. This recorder, as yours should, has the capacity to operate on 110-volt house current, on disposable batteries, or on a rechargeable battery pack. Like most cassette recorders, it has a built-in microphone but permits the attachment of an optional handheld mike (at a small extra cost).

Here are a few tips to follow in evaluating a recorder before purchasing: Place the machine on the store counter, set it on "record," and talk into it while standing close to the microphone. You might simply count to ten in a conversational tone. Facing the mike, place yourself about a foot away and prepare to step backwards. In something slightly louder than a conversational tone, say, "I am now one foot away." Then back up about a foot and say, "I am now two feet away," continuing this process through several repetitions. Use the store's facilities to record some music, and tape a few minutes' worth of casual conversation with the clerk.

If there are extraneous sounds in the store during your test run, so much the better. While playing the tape back, you will be able to determine the machine's directional capability by contrasting the voice on which the mike is trained with the diffused background noises.

The portability of your tape recorder is an important matter to consider, for the collector often spends several hours at a stretch carrying it about. At home it does not matter how heavy the machine; but away from home, often literally out in the field, the importance of weight is second only to the quality of sound reproduction. The latter is also determined by the quality of the tape used.

As a folklorist, you will soon find yourself on very intimate terms with your tape recorder. It should have no quirks to annoy you or shortcomings that might interfere with the success of your interviews or your attempts to record folk music. As soon as you get it home, experiment with your tape recorder every chance you get. People who learn to play folk instruments like fiddles, banjos, and dulcimers know their "axes" so well that they don't have to think twice about what they're doing. They seem to become one with their instrument. As a folklore collector, you must become one with your instrument, the tape recorder.

Recording tape: When buying cassette recording tape, consider three things: purpose, quality, and length. Only if your purpose is to get the best possible reproduction of a musical event should you even consider splurging on the most expensive grade of audio tape. In such an event, a knowledgeable salesperson can be trusted to sell you the type of cassette that will best suit your needs, without necessarily selling you the most expensive grade of tape in stock.

For the purpose of recording talk rather than music, almost any brand available in the medium price range—the kind of "low noise, high output" cassettes that come with their own plastic cases—will do nicely. Avoid the low-grade, unboxed varieties that come packaged with several in a plastic bag. They're fine for small children to amuse themselves with, but they are unsuitable for your purposes as a folklore collector.

Consideration should be given to the matter of recording length of the cassette tapes purchased. On one hand, whether the recorded event be a conversation, a narrative, or a musical performance, less than thirty minutes of recording time on each side of the tape will be too brief. Either the flow of talk will have to be interrupted too frequently or an important segment might be lost while the cassette is being turned over or changed. On the other hand, although tapes are available with an hour of recording time on each side, these are not generally recommended. Since all cassettes are the same size, it stands to reason that a longer tape will take up more room than a shorter one on the reels inside the casing. The longer tapes are therefore more likely to drag or to break because they are wound more tightly. Your best bets are the cassettes with thirty minutes per side (C60) or those with forty-five minutes per side (C90). It is a good idea to use the same time-length tapes consistently. That way you'll soon know automatically when to change tape.

Photographs and Slides

Folklore should be seen as well as heard, but you don't have to be a topnotch photographer to make satisfactory use of a camera in your folklore gathering. If you're not a graphic artist, it is strongly recommended that you make use of a camera as enthusiastically as the tape recorder. The two devices make perfect complements, and you will probably soon begin to discover that your new awareness of folklore has broadened the scope of your pictorial eye.

The least desirable sort of photo to include in your collection is the color snapshot, as it will deteriorate too rapidly. Folklore is for the time of your life, remember? So you're better off shooting either black-and-white photos or color (or black-and-white) slides. Black-and-white exposures will last more than a lifetime. Color slides can be stored so as to insure their relative permanence.

As an all-around amateur with respect to folklore collecting, you should not have to undertake more than you can manage. Keep the picture-taking simple. If this is your first photography venture, use a cartridge-loaded, pocket-size camera—the look-and-shoot variety. What you want on your pictures are clear and true images. The next best equipment would be a small camera that lets you make adjustments for distance from the focus of attention. That way you can take better close-ups of artifacts as well as hands and faces.

It is possible to enjoy slides even if you don't own a screen and projector. There are many inexpensive slide-viewing gadgets on the market. Some have to be held up to a source of light and others contain a built-in light, but all serve to enlarge the image just enough to insure pleasant viewing by one person. Even if you do own a projector, such a device makes previewing a set of slides quick and easy.

An individual slide viewer that operates on house current (no batteries), that sits on a table, and that has a built-in light source is preferable. If it also has two trays—one on each side of the center—your job becomes even easier. The right-hand tray holds a stack of slides to be fed into the viewer by means of push-pull panel; the left-hand tray catches the slides as they leave the viewer and stacks them neatly.

Maintenance and Storage

What may seem like placing the cart before the horse, since presumably you don't yet have a collection that requires maintenance and storage, is merely an attempt to practice an ounce of prevention. You might as well know how to treat your collection before you begin.

Cards and papers should be kept dust free and protected from dampness, mildew, and prolonged exposure to strong light. Common sense will lead you in the right directions. Shoe boxes are fine for filing cards. Manila folders, or better yet, manila envelopes make fine receptacles for sets of papers including cards, clippings, audio tapes, and even photographs—all dealing with a particular topic or interview. Clean cartons with lids make good improvised filing cabinets.

Should you ever strike it rich and/or become passionately serious about your collection, then it's time to try to obtain the kinds of acid-free folders, boxes, and envelopes that are used by libraries and institutional archives to preserve valuable documents and photographs. Librarians can offer suggestions for you as to materials and sources.

Audio tapes: As you probably know, a previously taped recording can be erased simply by being run through the recorder while the "record" and "play" buttons are simultaneously depressed. But you will never be depressed about having accidentally erased a favorite folklore tape if you will (*after* you have made your recording) take a retracted ball-point pen and push in the little plastic tabs located on the surface of the cassette opposite the exposed strip of recording tape. The right tab controls side one; the left tab controls side two. This operation is reversible. If you should wish to erase a tape, after all, just cover each tab slot with plastic mending tape. The cassette will now re-record—just as if you had not pushed in the tabs.

Fill out the labels on each side of the tape cassette, using a permanent marker pen. Identify each side by content and situation: the who (speakers or musicians), the occasion (Texas Arts & Crafts Fair, for example), the place (Kerrville, Texas), and the date recorded (May 28, 1978). If more than two sides of cassettes are used for a single recording session, use the marker pen to number the sides consecutively.

If you've had any experience with sound tapes, you have probably heard it said many times that playback is good for them. Here's why. No one really knows the life-span of a magnetic tape, simply because they are too recent an invention. What can happen to a tape is similar in many respects to the deterioration that occurs when an old plastic bag suffers after long exposure to dust, dampness, heat, and light. It loses pliability and snaps easily. You can prevent such deterioration in your tapes if you understand the minimal requirements for their care.

Playback alone—at least annually—can prevent a multitude of problems. It will prevent a tape from reaching the point where it might stick to itself permanently. Periodical playback will also reduce the chances of having the oxide, or magnetic coating, flake off a tape that has fallen into disuse, and prevent the possibility of imprints from one layer of a tape to another. This can occur if a tape should accidentally become too tightly wound.

A conscious effort at taking good care of tapes when you first begin to build your collection will free you from having to think twice about it later. Up to the time of this writing none of the tapes in my own collection have shown any evidence of deteriorating, and some of these are more than ten years old. All are stored at home under quite average temperature and humidity conditions.

Store tapes in their plastic cases. If you wish, you can write a brief identifying notation on adhesive tape affixed to any case that cannot be seen through. Stand tapes on edge during storage. It helps to keep their magnetic coating intact. Do not place cassettes in metal containers or cabinets. Keep them on wooden or plastic (any nonmetallic) shelves. If a metal storage unit should become magnetized—and metal is susceptible to that—it could de-magnetize your tapes or otherwise adversely affect the composition of their magnetic coating.

Photographs and slides: You may, of course, keep your photographs in albums. Numerous varieties protect each picture behind some sort of clear plastic shield—the self-adhering kind as well as the envelope type. However, because you may want to organize your folklore collection photographs differently than you would a family album, it is recommended that you stock up on "refills" and forget about the albums themselves. Then you will be able to store sets of photos together with other documents that refer to the same subject.

For example, you might want all your photos of traditional basketry to be stored together. On the other hand, you might decide to store the photos depicting one particular basket maker's processes in one manila envelope, together with your notes on the subject and your taped interviews with the craftsperson. However you decide to arrange sets of collected documents, keep photos out of strong light, free from dust, and anchored against sturdy cardboard backing to prevent their curling up.

Slides should be stored in boxes and prevented from scratching each other's surfaces. Unlike tapes, slides may be stored in metal containers. Storage containers for slides come in cardboard, plastic, or metal, infrequently in wood. You might like to get ambitious and make some wooden ones. What they all have in common are grooves or partitions which allow each slide to stand separately.

The better to enjoy your harvest: Having fun *having,* not just making your collection of folklore documents—writings, recordings, and pictures—is what it's all about. Use a little common sense about taking care of these items. Figure out a good way to store them, not only for their own protection, but also to enable you to find what you want when you want something out of your collection. Do not get so hung up on maintenance and storage that you forget the reason you're writing those recollections, recording those inter- views, and taking those pictures—for the terrific enjoyment they will bring you and those with whom you care to share them. So arrange to make a collection you won't hesitate to use.

Play back your tapes—*soon* and *periodically*—for reasons other than maintenance. *Soon,* because you'll get ideas for follow-up questions before you lose contact with an interviewee and while the topics discussed are still fresh in both your minds. Note further questions in writing. Don't trust your memory to recall every query that came to you as you listened to the playback.

Periodically, because you will learn from each interview you conduct. Once enough time has passed to give you the perspective needed to be objective about your work, you will be able to recognize your shortcomings as an interviewer and will turn out to be your own best teacher. You'll be able to tell if you're doing too much of the talking, if you have a tendency to interrupt a speaker prematurely, and how well you guide an informant back to a topic of interest to you if he or she veers off course before you're ready for a change in direction.

Playing back your tapes periodically has further merits. Not only will you become a good self-critic so that your interviewing will become progressively more competent, but you will also get so used to the sound of your own voice (and the person past the age of four doesn't exist who likes the sound of his own voice on tape—at first) that you'll lose all self-consciousness and false modesty and begin to enjoy sharing the tapes with others.

Moreover, you'll get a tremendous kick out of listening to your interviews. It can even be more fun than watching television or listening to the radio because it's material that you produced and are especially interested in. It certainly requires less effort to slip an audio cassette into a tape player than to have to set up projector and screen for viewing slides and home movies—unless your home is spacious enough to accommodate having such equipment permanently out and ready for use. Best of all, like a good book, a taped interview or musical performance will yield something new in the way of revelation or insight each time you return to it.

Workshop on wheels: A good place to listen to playbacks is in your car, especially when you're driving alone. Even if your car is not equipped to play cassettes, you can bring your portable tape recorder with you. As soon as you can, jot down any follow-up questions that are fresh on your mind.

While we're on the subject of the automobile, it wouldn't be a bad idea to keep a pen, some 4" x 6" cards, a couple of rolls of film, and a few blank cassettes in the glove compartment of your car, providing that your car doesn't spend much time parked in extreme heat.

Youthful bike riders or elderly pedestrians might bear in mind that backpacks, lockable storage containers on bikes, or personally owned shopping baskets on wheels make good portable workshops, too.

The folklore gatherer who gets the best harvest is the one who adopts the traditional Boy Scout motto, attempting always to Be Prepared. You never know what treasures lie around the corner, so you might as well have with you whatever you might need to record a find. Usually 4" x 6" cards will suffice, but try to avoid the "how-I-wish-I-had-my-camera-along" syndrome.

And now for our first interview.

Conducting Your First Interview

U sing a tape recorder to collect folklore in the format of oral biography is especially rewarding. This interviewing activity touches on family folklore and the folklife of the community at the same time that it focuses on the word-for-word narrative of the life of an individual bearer of folk traditions. An oral biography is obtained cumulatively, over several recording sessions.

Nothing succeeds like the combination of an interviewer who is interested in and at ease with an informant plus an interviewee who is equally relaxed with the interviewer. The ideal situation for a folklore collector's first interviewing experience would be that of grandchild-as-interviewer and grandparent-as-interviewee. Rapport between speaker and listener is built in. The situation is anxiety free and bound to produce a flow of tradition-rich reminiscences. Therefore, go and interview your grandmother.

Even if you have spent a lot of time with your grandmother, when you approach her with this new project, listen to her accounts very carefully. Even often-heard stories will become objects of your respect.

What's that? You don't have a living grandparent, let alone a grandmother? Then go and interview someone else's grandmother or grandfather. The term *grandmother* is, of course, symbolic. It could be taken to mean "grandfather," "great aunt," or "the man across the street"—someone old enough to be your grandparent.

Elderly folks make wonderful interviews. Their memories of the past are usually crystal clear. Not only do they generally enjoy recollecting the past—more so than a younger person, who is busily trying to cope with the over-booked present—but if you have never been exposed to the life-style of a person two generations removed from your own, you're in for a surprising treat.

Really? You are a grandparent yourself? Well, in that case, either interview a peer or interview yourself. Oh? You would feel awkward sitting alone talking to yourself? You have three choices: (1) Do it anyway. Once you get started, you'll lose your sense of awkwardness and find yourself enjoying the experience. (2) Invite someone to come over to be your interviewer. Get that person hooked on collecting, too. (3) Or write a letter to your grandchildren—a long letter—one with many installments.

Unless you live in the same household as your interviewee, it's always a good idea to phone a few days ahead requesting permission to visit; then follow up by calling to confirm an appointment.

Ordinarily, you may be anything but a paragon of punctuality. But when it comes to visiting someone confined to house or bed, make an extra effort to arrive exactly at the time promised. Understandably, folks who are shut in especially look forward to the arrival of visitors and tend to become upset if one is tardy.

Taking your informant's normal routine into consideration, limit your visits or recording sessions to an approximate maximum of an hour and a half. Schedule your visits one at a time, no more than a week, preferably only a few days apart. Both of you will enjoy the experience best if the momentum and the narrative continuity are maintained.

Interviewing Techniques

An interviewer who has to fiddle with the tape recorder, fuss with the microphone, or fumble with cassettes is likely to be ill at ease and make the informant uncomfortable, too. Therefore, for smooth sailing during any interview, rehearse these simple steps until you almost know them in your sleep.

Before the interview: (1) Practice turning and changing cassettes until you are adept at it. (2) Be equally adept at changing rolls of film or film cartridges in your camera. (3) Test the machine, micro-phone, batteries, and tape in a single operation, by counting into your tape recorder with, then again without, house current, using the cassette on which you plan to record during your next interview. (4) Check your camera to make sure any batteries still work. Test the flash mechanism if you plan to use it. (5) Label at least one cassette with the informant's name and the date of the interview, as well as by number. Make it a habit to number consecutively all the cassettes in a series of interviews with the same informant. (6) Remove the cellophane or any other outer wrapping from extra cassettes you anticipate using. (7) Load film into your camera. (8) Have on hand: (a) more recording tape than you think you'll need and a fresh set of batteries or power pack, (b) extra camera film and flash bulbs (if used), and (c) a household extension cord—so that you can place the recorder where you want it if you are running on house current.

At the outset you must decide where to place the recorder, including the microphone. You want the machine where you can easily monitor the reels and reach over to turn or change cassettes. You want the microphone aimed directly at the informant, neither so close up that the interviewee can't possibly ignore it nor so far away that soft-spoken words might fail to register clearly. So long as you speak up, the machine will pick up your questions even if you are not facing the mike directly yourself.

If, on the one hand, you are using the built-in condenser microphone, then you and the interviewee might sit side by side or at right angles at a kitchen, dining room, or bridge table, with the recorder between you. Or, you might position the recorder between you on a piece of furniture the height of a lamp table.

But when there is no convenient furniture on which to set the recorder, sit close-by, holding the recorder in one propped hand (especially easy to do if you own the compact, lightweight machine suggested earlier).

If, on the other hand, you are using a separate mike—the inexpensive, serviceable kind that plugs into the machine—place the recorder anywhere for your convenience. Rather than hand hold the mike—either aiming it awkwardly in the speaker's face (like a roving reporter) or, worse, waving it back and forth between yourself and your interviewee—drape it over your shoulder.

A piece of adhesive tape or a small safety pin (around, not through, the wire) can serve to anchor the mike to your clothing, to keep it from slipping below shoulder height. So long as you have placed yourself within conversational range of the person you're interviewing, the mike at your shoulder will pick up both sides of the dialogue beautifully, especially as the speaker looks your way while talking.

As soon as you believe the machine and mike to be well positioned, fast forward the tape long enough to get the plastic leader out of the way and conduct a brief test. With the mike turned on, ask your interviewee to please count to ten in a conversational tone. If both of you can clearly be heard on playback, you'll know that all systems are go.

Try to make attentive listening and eye contact with your informant your primary concern; monitoring the tape recorder should come second—providing that you've done your homework.

If you must change tapes in the midst of an interesting account, you may have to ask your interviewee to back up so that there is no gap on the tape. It is better, therefore, to take advantage of any lull in conversation shortly before all the tape has run out, changing or turning cassettes during the hiatus.

Conducting an informal interview: Always go into any interview situation with a few prepared questions listed on a notepad or 4" x 6" card. An informative interview with your grandmother, how-ever, is bound to conduct itself. That's one reason why an oral biography is to become your first venture into the field of informal interviewing.

In this case, base your prepared questions on either or both: what you already know about your grandmother that you would now like to record, as in, "I'd like to hear that story again about the time you . . . ," and what you don't know about her life that you'd be interested in learning, as in, "Come to think of it, Grandmother, I know nothing at all about your teenage years." Chances are, though, that you're not going to need most of your ready-made questions.

With surprisingly little effort on your part, someone like your grandmother becomes launched on a veritable stream of recollections. It is best, therefore, to keep direct questions to a minimum. Asking just the first usually prompts answers to the rest as well.

Try not to interrupt the flow of conversation. Digressions sometimes produce the most interesting accounts of all, so make sure your informant is really far afield before deliberately steering a line of talk back on course.

Remember that you have come to interview someone other than yourself. Don't get carried away with your own response-making tendency. Talk only to elicit responses. When no such stimulus is necessary, maintain your good listener's role. Look alive, nod vigorously at times, but bear in mind that too many vocal assents tend to cover up the ends or beginnings of an informant's recorded sentences—as one can discover when playing back an interview.

You will want to ask some questions, not so much the ones you brought along to get your interview moving, but those that derive spontaneously from specific topics covered in the narrative. As these occur to you, jot them down on a handy index card so that you won't forget what you wished to know, and wait for a lull in the interviewee's associative train of thought. One caution remains, however: sometimes lulls just mean that the speaker is thinking— collecting more thoughts. Short periods of silence should not concern you. Leave the recorder running; give your informant a chance to think before attempting to move the narration along.

If openings are few and far between, and you have several questions to ask, save them for the tail end of the interview, time permitting. Should time run out before you can cover them all, begin the next interview-visit with the leftovers. Listen to your tapes immediately after each session, because it can also happen on playback that you notice gaps in thought not previously apparent to you. On subsequent visits, you can get your interviewee to supply clarifying details.

Interviewing Your Grandmother

Mary W. Harper, who has no children, let alone grandchildren, but who would be a fine grandmother if she did, has been elected to be the grandmother representative in this book. Portions to follow of a series of interviews with her epitomize all the conditions that you will find when you interview your own grandmother: relaxed enjoyment, a continuous flow of narration by reason of the association of ideas, and a wealth of recollections which bespeak folk traditions.

Adaptation to print: Not only what is said, but the way in which it is said is of utmost significance to the folklore collector. Therefore, any interview loses dimension on the printed page. The sounds of the voice—its emotional range, its unique inflections, and its regional way of pronouncing words—are terrifically important aspects of the whole experience of an interview. What you won't be able to perceive here, for example, is the animation in Mrs. Harper's voice, the pace, the music of emphatically stressed syllables at varied intervals.

But you will be able to take in the speaker's exact words. The collector is never interested in altering or revising an interview for style, that is, for sentence construction, or choices in grammar and vocabulary. To do so would be to defeat one's purposes as a "recorder"; we are neither censors nor literary stylists. For, when it comes to recording folklore, the beauty of the expression lies in its authenticity.

Recollections by Mary W. Harper: Mary Harper possesses the gift of the narrator—a talent not uncommon among Southerners. Only, hers has been especially nurtured by years of experience, during the thirties, on the lecture platform. Her life has been full and good: her marriage—exemplary, her career—rewarding, her childhood—a folklore collector's delight.

Born in 1894, Mary Harper, née Mary Sue Wigley, grew up on Sand Mountain in DeKalb County, Alabama. Let's listen to her tell about it:

I grew up in the southern Appalachian mountains, where we never had any mining or slaves. It was all agricultural, you know. I was a young woman in my mid-teens before I saw a high school or library or a railroad or a black man.

I lived in a log house until I was six or seven. My father was a country merchant and a postmaster. Dad had a post office which failed. Rural free delivery put him out. And then he sold goods on time, and the store failed also. One of those bad years came along, and he couldn't collect his debts.

A lot of people in Sand Mountain got penned up there in agricultural Appalachia, because they didn't have any mining. They just stayed there. It was so isolated that they didn't get out and go places. They carried on the traditions of England.

Sand Mountain where I grew up used to be the happy hunting ground for the Cherokee Indians, and no white people were up there. When I grew up it wasn't thickly settled like it is now; it was thinly settled. In fact, none of the white folks was born on the mountain. They were born in the valley.

I remember the Indian songs I used to sing. My grandmother had Indians for neighbors, and after she learned 'em, my mother learned them from her. Then I just learned them from my mother. One goes like this [singing]:

> *CHEE'PA SAY'LA WEH S'NAH-GA*
> *KȲ WON HȲ HEY-HEY*
> *CHEE'PA SAY'LA WEH S'NAH-GA*
> *NAH KȲ'TOH MAH-GA*
>
> *AND-A KȲ TOH MAH-GA*
> *AN'-A KȲ TOH MAH-GA*
>
> *CHEE'PA SAY'LA WEH S'NAH-GA*
> *KȲ WON HȲ HEY-HEY*
> *CHEE'PA SAY'LA WEH S'NAH-GA*
> *NAH KȲ TOH MAH-GA*

That one's really pretty. I don't know what it means; I don't know a word of it. Back when I could sing better than I can now, they had me to record 'em over to the University.

When recording an oral biography, you want to know as much as you can about the *narrator's ancestry,* and *time and place of birth.* It is logical for those subjects to come up at the beginning. However, there is no fixed order to any of the points which are to be covered. Nor is each one neatly completed in its own stretch of narration.

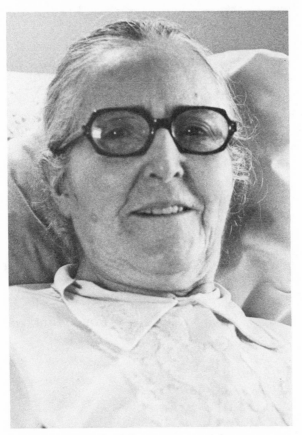

Mary Harper possesses the gift of the narrator—a talent not uncommon among Southerners. Only, hers has been especially nurtured by years of experience, during the thirties, on the lecture platform. Her life has been full and good; her marriage—exemplary, her career—rewarding, her childhood—a folklore collector's delight.

Such topics as *father's occupation, mother's activities,* and *place of birth* may be ongoing, as they are in the present interview.

You would ask questions one at a time, however, questions like, *Since church-going was an important part of your up-bringing, what are some of your earliest memories of religion?*

Dad used to take me to church in his arms and walk three miles and he used to lead the singing, and I thought I had to sing too. But I didn't know the words. But I'd move my lips. And after church, my dad's friends would come up and shake my hand, tell me how they enjoyed my singing.

And as little as I was—in Dad's arms—I had a guilty conscience. Somebody said they didn't believe children that young had guilty consciences. But I felt like I ought to tell everyone, "I wasn't singin'; I was just movin' my lips!"

You would also ask, *How many brothers and sisters were in your family?* and *What were some of your favorite games and pastimes?* The former is a good question to elicit folk traditions, if they don't surface automatically, as they do in Mary Harper's recollections. You could also, of course, employ the folklore-gathering techniques presented earlier in this book. But Mrs. Harper recalls independently:

I was one of the older ones of nine children. It's funny how I can remember events when I was so young. We used to find these little holes in the sand—I can't think of what they called 'em.

Most Southern folks could remind her, "Doodle bug holes."

Doodle bugs. Yeah. And we'd get down right over the hole and say:

> *Doodle bug, doodle bug*
> *Fly away home.*
> *Your house is on fire*
> *Your babies will burn!*

You've heard that?

Yes, in variation, too. Some folks say, "Come and get your bread and milk" instead of "Your house is on fire." Young and old, all over the South, they get down on all fours, peer into those sandy mounds, and often blow gently into the holes to watch those strange beetles, no bigger than lady bugs, of indeterminate hue [like dirty sand], come poking out.

I can remember one game we used to play. It must have come from England. Did you ever hear of "Grandma Hobblegobble?" It sounds English, and it goes like this:

"Grandma Hobblegobble sent me to you, sir"
[reciting in a sing-songy tone like that which children adopt for jump rope rhymes].

We were five children then and Dad would say that to us. He'd be sittin' out in front of us. He was an unusual daddy. A lot of daddies don't have time to spend with their children. But he'd sit out in front of us, and he'd say,

"Grandma Hobblegobble sent me to you, sir."
And we'd say, in unison,
"Oh, what to do sir?"
And he'd say,
"Well, keep one hammer going like I do, sir."
And then he'd do this [pantomiming the gestures of making a hammer go up and down with the right hand]. And then he'd say it again, and we'd say, "Oh, what to do sir?" and he'd say, "Keep two hammers going like I do, sir." So then, we'd all be with two hammers [the left and right hands going up and down as though wielding two hammers].

And then he'd come again with "Grandma Hobblegobble sent me to you, sir," and we'd say, "What to do sir?" and then he'd go knocking up and down with one foot—two hands and one foot. And then, the fourth time, he'd say, "Keep four hammers going like I do, sir." And we'd all keep our four "hammers" going. The fifth time around he'd say, "Well, keep five hammers going, like I do, sir." And then he would do his head up and down that way [nodding vigorously].

And then the sixth time around, he'd say, "Well, keep six hammers going like I do, sir." And he'd stick out his tongue. Mrs. Harper demonstrates by making her tongue go in and out in rapid succession, at which the interviewer begins to laugh. Still in control of her own mirth, but barely, she continues by explaining that the game would usually end with the children's laughter at their dad's antics.

We used to jump rope, and I could go in backwards or forwards. I could go in when the rope was coming down or going over.

They had cotton ropes for the plow lines, but they were too valuable to let us play and wear 'em out making jump ropes of of them. So we had to go to the woods and get cross vines off of trees.

It's sort of a three-cornered vine—three-cornered rope. They grew in swampy places, and they'd stick to a tree just as tight as they could hold till they got up to the top to where any leaves were on it. And we'd pull it down. It took a lot of strength to pull it down.

We used to smoke them and make our mouths sore. We could split it into three pieces. Just lit one end, put the end that wasn't lighted in our mouths, and sucked the porous wood where the smoke would come up through it.

Did it taste good?

I think we were just pushed for something to do. It didn't taste like tobacco.

During an interview such as this one, the collector would want to know *how special holidays were celebrated* in the family during the narrator's childhood.

We didn't have much money for Christmas presents, so Mother would make cookies and make them like dolls. She'd put raisins for their eyes and mark off something for the mouths. And they'd be pretty cookies that way.

And then we had our homemade molasses candy. We'd pull it until it would change color and then twist it. Oh, it was good candy, too. And we'd have tops made out of spools that we could wind up with a string and dash down on the floor. They would put all that kind of stuff in our stockings.

Dad and Mother usually let us hang our stockings up two nights. Candy didn't cost much in those days—a dime's worth would be nearly a pound of stick candy. We had lots of fun if we didn't have any money—back in those days.

The interviewer would also want to know about the narrator's *childhood school experiences.* As related here, these can yield unexpected insights into the folklife of the community:

Back in the old days they didn't have enough money to have schools in Alabama. They would have a school in this community one year, and the next year they would have it in another community. Sometimes it wouldn't come back to this first community for about four years. The first school I went to was where I attended church. It was at Russ Chapel.

I was six years old when I started to school, and I can remember I was my dad's tomboy. I used to say about my dad, "He liked to whistle and sing and grow cotton." I learned how to whistle. And when Dad in the field wanted something, he would just whistle to you, and you could hear him a mile. So we'd know to take him some water. So I learned to whistle.

And when I went to school that first day, they tried to scare me to death. They called me "Chatterbox," I was such a bad kid to talk. They had me afraid to say anything for fear I'd get switched.

So I had to take my seat on a church bench, and my feet wouldn't touch the floor. I got awfully tired of swinging my feet up in the air. Everything was so quiet, I couldn't stand it any longer. So I whistled just as loud as I could!

The principal looked up to see, "Now who was that?" I knew my time had come. I was frightened to death. He could tell by looking at me who it was, I'm pretty sure, and some of the boys pointed over to my side.

It was segregated, you know, back in the old days. The males had to sit on one side and females on the other, unless you was courtin'. Courting couples could take either side they wanted to. They made allowances for the courtin' couples.

So these boys pointed over to my seat. But I think the principal must have had a little girl of his own, because he didn't even get after me.

I can remember when we used to have those homemade traps in the log house. We had a window on each side of the chimney, and come a big snowstorm—and on this mountain that was twelve hundred feet above sea level, we had more snow—Dad would stay in the window with his string on a cob or something. The birds were hungry, and he'd put a little seed under the trap, you know. It'd get full of birds.

In a while he'd pull the string, pull the trigger, and that would make the trap fall real quickly. And he'd go out and turn the little birds loose and keep the partridges. And we'd have a chicken pie out of partridges. They were quail, you know, and they were good eating too.

The interviewer never knows what interesting information might come to the fore when the narrator is given her lead. When Mrs. Harper talks about a frightening childhood experience, the folklore collector learns about "the wet weather wash place" as accidentally as ten-year-old Mary Wigley discovered it in a storm:

I can remember being in a swamp getting a cross vine one time. All of a sudden came a loud clap of thunder, and I started to run, trying to get home—I wasn't more than ten years old.

And I got into a trail that had a pretty big old white oak tree by the side of it. And I remember saying out loud to myself, "Well, I know I've never seen this before." But I turned my head and looked the other way, and there was our wet weather wash place!

Yes, it *was* only used during wet weather, the interviewer learns when inquiring about it later (having made a note to do so when Mrs. Harper first mentioned it):

The main thing was the battling block—a stump that wouldn't split, that was sawed off even and big enough until they could put it down on the ground. And then it'd have a battlin' stick. I can remember how they'd use this lye soap made from the ashes, and they'd use a stick and battle on the clothes—not too hard. But they'd get it real soapy—full of soap—and then they'd put it over in the tub and rinse it. It was kind of rough on the clothes at best, but of course the clothes weren't flabby.

That was when adult women used the shimmy [chemise] and bought unbleached muslin by the bolt to make their curtains. My mother wore a shimmy as long as she lived. She always wore her dresses pretty long, too, about a foot from the floor.

I wore linsey dresses. And one reason we wore those wool clothes was that we had to get our heat from log fires and big fireplaces. And any kind of a cotton cloth or somethin' like that was in danger of getting in the fire and burning up. So we had the kind of clothes that wouldn't ignite easily.

Even the cotton things were a whole lot heavier if they were woven at home. I've seen my aunt Nona weave cloth. But my mother used to spin, and they'd always have wool and cotton thread, both, mixed together because wool wasn't strong enough by itself.

Family stories often center on eccentric characters. No interviewer collecting oral biography should neglect to inquire about the existence of *"characters"* memorable to the narrator's family.

In Mary Harper's case it was her Uncle Alfred. *You just couldn't fill him up—he had such a big appetite. And people always had quarterly meetings where they'd bring out dinner. And Uncle Alfred always went to all of them. He'd get his hands full and eat and eat and eat. And I remember my father and mother wouldn't let us laugh at him.*

Three questions, which may be separately asked, usually prompt the most fascinating childhood reminiscences and folkloric details of all: (1) *Was there anything you were forbidden to do as a child?* (2) *Were there places you were not allowed to go?* (3) *What were your greatest childhood fears?*

Now, my dad was a good rock thrower. He grew up in Georgia where they had little flint rocks—just the nicest things to throw. And he had learned to throw accurately and kill squirrels and rabbits.

I can remember one time I had me a pretty playhouse under a tree, where Dad had a lot of wooden poles placed around, until it made a complete tent. Dad called me, and he didn't bother to explain it might be dangerous—if one log fell, the whole business would fall. He just said, "Now, you can't play here anymore." I was awfully mad at him, and I ran away to this swamp full of little ol' trails that had been made by our sheep that ran outdoors.

And I hadn't been down there long until the rocks began to fall down close to me. And I thought, "Now, I've been a bad girl. I ran away from my dad, and God's throwin' rocks at me." Then I remembered that Mother always told us that God loved us. So I changed. "No," I said, "it's the booger man throwing rocks at me." That scared me still worse. They had me scared of the booger man. We weren't allowed to say "devil," but he was the booger man, you know; that's what was really meant.

It didn't take me long to take a notion to come out of that swamp. And I went-a running back to the house, but the rocks just kept a-hummin', getting a little closer to me. I ran back to the house, and there was Dad puttin' the harness on the mule, laughing. He was just tickled that he had scared me out of my swamp.

Such is the material that family saga, the handed-down family legendry, is made of.

Another fear takes the interview back into the spheres of family saga, occupations, and childrens' pastimes:

We didn't have bears in our country. But I was afraid of bears, and we used to pretend we were more afraid of them than we were. Dad and Mother were busy counting stamps for the post office, and they wanted us out of the way. My job was to take care of Ruth, my sister just younger than I was. The first big June apple trees had spreading limbs, and we'd go down there after it got dark. And there would be a big black spot, you know, where the limbs was thicker in some spots than they were in others. So I'd take Ruth down there to that apple tree, and I'd say, "Now, do you see that big black bear up in that apple tree?"

And Ruth would go to screaming at the top of her voice. You could hear her to the next neighborhood. And I could outrun her. I'd get back to the house quicker than she could. And then, just as soon as she got back, she'd pull my sleeve and say, "Now, scare me again!"

An oral biography does not stop with childhood. The collector might inquire about social activities for adolescents during the narrator's teens. Mary Wigley's adolescence was without frivolity, as her reminiscences about her fourteenth year demonstrate. A good question to raise during the recording of years beyond childhood is a twofold one: *What expectations did your parents have you for you, and what were your expectations for yourself?* Mary Harper covers both topics in one response:

I had a lot of freedom of choice when I grew up because my mother wasn't trying to get her girls married. They had big families back then, the land was poor, and she knew the hard times women had. She was a very inspiring woman, and she encouraged us to get a good education. I remember in one of my speeches dealing with the economic problems of the home, I made the statement that "all the dollar-saving plans I've learned through the years of forced economy sink into insignificance in value by the side of the lessons in faith and courage I learned from a cheerful mother while we were desperately poor."

We were so poor, you know, after we lost our home at the "store place." The man that was furnishing Dad's store was bad to take over land of the people. That was his style; he had a mortgage on our home and wanted all the land he could get. So he took over our home. We didn't have anything left except one mule and a cow and a sewing machine, but they were all mortgaged too. I used to be afraid of the sound of approaching wheels for fear he was sending after our things.

There wasn't any land left for homesteading. Dad was in debt and he wouldn't go anywhere [for help] because he had been a leader in the community. We'd been better off than the neighbors, but now we were poorer than anybody in the community.

We had to move out on a rented farm when I was around fourteen. I felt very upset to be on rented land. All my friends were on their own places. I stopped and watched the sunrise on top of Lookout Mountain, and then I ran to the house that morning. I had a sudden inspiration and wrote down on paper what I was going to do.

First was to study at home and make a teacher. And second was to help Dad pay the debts, 'cause he didn't have any idea about getting out of paying them. I knew that debts had to be paid. Then I was going to help buy them another home. And the fourth thing was, I was going to graduate from college.

After each one I wrote, "Did I?" And then I told myself over and over again for years that I couldn't possibly die happy until all four questions were answered with "yes," and then finally I believed it.

This determined, very young woman accomplished all her goals and more:

I didn't wait to go about it. That was the day I started studying at home to make a teacher. Had to study in the cotton seed house to get away from the kids. And I learned enough until I could take the state teachers' examination. You didn't have to know much to teach school in Alabama then. I was seventeen years old when I began teaching.

Back in those old days they thought it took a man to control a school. So I was an assistant, getting thirty dollars a month for my salary. I paid ten dollars a month for both room and board.

A hard-shell Baptist preacher was the principal. One day there was some kind of church gathering, and he left his pupils in my charge. There was one real bad boy, the worst in the community—he had the reputation. And as soon as the principal left, he got to walking the floor back and forth. And I'd tell him to go back to his seat, and he wouldn't pay any attention to me.

I was up on the high stage, like they had back then. It took about four steps to get to the top. Finally, this bad boy started climbing the steps to the platform where I was. I guess he thought he could frighten me. I had the principal's switch that he used for a pointer at the blackboard—that Baptist preacher didn't whip children; he'd just get down and pray for 'em. The boy just kept a-coming, climbing the steps slowly, and I wasn't in any notion to pray. And as he got close to me, I just landed on his legs and switched him good.

He was so surprised and so shocked that he just went straight to his seat without talking back. I didn't know if I'd be fired when the principal got back because I didn't have any authority to whip his pupils. But when he came back, he didn't say a word to me. And I just kept my mouth shut.

But the news got out. And it got into the next county where they had a school called Union. And those trustees got together and said, "You know, I believe that woman could control a school as well as any man." So they doubled my salary and paid me fifty-nine dollars a month to move close to Boaz and teach their school.

Special skills and interests is another topic that should be included in an oral biography. In Mary Wigley's case she changed from teaching school to being a home demonstration agent. *I didn't have a bit of college education yet. I got a school down there on the Coosa River, and we had a two-acre playground. One side of it, a narrow strip, had gone up in sagebrush. People used to make brooms out of it in the old days.*

I divided it into twelve by twelve feet plots and let every child have a plot that wanted it. That was during World War I when they had wheatless days and had to take cornbread to school. So we planted things in our garden—greens—that we could cook to eat with our cornbread. And we'd invite the mail carrier or just anybody that would to come eat with us. Now, hot school lunches was almost unheard of in those days.

Hastings was the biggest seed man in the South—Burpee was in the North. After I sent him some of the publicity the Wetumpka Herald *gave us about our garden and school lunches, he thought I ought to be a home demonstration agent, and so he recommended me to the Georgia folks.*

When I got through with this six-week course in Atlanta, the state agency in Alabama offered me Cullman County and furnished me with a horse and buggy. And there wasn't a mile of paved road in that county that wasn't made out of gravel. That old horse would get gravel in his foot every so often and have to walk on three legs, limping mighty bad. I'd have to take him to the blacksmith's shop to have the thing taken out. I drove that old horse for sixteen months before I got a car.

Education: Remarkably well educated for an Appalachian woman of the early 1900s, Mary Wigley earned a Bachelor's degree from

Oklahoma A&M at Stillwater (now Oklahoma State University) and a Master's from Columbia College in Chicago in economic problems of the home. She lectured on the subject during the thirties. *While some people were jumpin from high windows, I was earning a good living telling folks about forward planning and encouraging them to go back to the land.*

Another good interviewing technique, especially with a less fluent narrator than Mary Harper, involves *looking at a family photo album* and taping the interviewee's associations with the pictures. An interviewer might also *inquire whether the informant ever kept a diary or journal.* Mary Harper went one better. She wrote her autobiography:

I didn't write it until my husband died in 1966. I call it "Wind from the East." Dad used to call us before daybreak with this warning: "The wind is from the east this morning." And we wouldn't wait to be called a second time. He said that because the wind from the east usually meant rain. Sometimes in these prolonged rainy spells an hour's work of picking cotton was equivalent to a half a day's work afterward.

Her *courtship and* a relatively late *marriage* are not yet part of the autobiographical text. But it makes a fine oral tale:

I was married in '42, at the beginning of World War II. I married a noted botanist from the state of Maine. When he started to come South for the first time, people up North asked him, "Sir, are you going to the South to teach botany?" And he said, "No, I'm going down there to practice it." He had more than twenty plants in Alabama named for him, and he discovered over two hundred. My husband was a good man. He never did speak a sharp word to me. He was very Southern in his attitudes even though he was born in Maine.

They used to tell me when I was studying before I got my Master's degree, when I'd run up on something I'd want to know about the South, "Now, you write to Dr. Roland M. Harper." He'd answer my letter, but he never would keep up the correspondence. He'd heard me speak in 1936 at the University of Alabama. It was a big crowd, I remember, and he came up and spoke to me afterwards. But I didn't hear anything from him for eight years.

I wrote him a letter one cold February night. And I got quite personal with him and asked him how did it happen he just never did get married. And I reckon he thought I wasn't immune to being interested. He had just been relieved of taking care of his mother, and he never had had enough money to support a wife. But he didn't wait.

He walked out to our house. He pretended that he wanted to be walking. He walked all over Alabama. He didn't have a car. There was a plant he wanted to look up at Collinsville in the valley, and so he walked from Collinsville out to where we lived. I can remember seein' him come down the road. He had kind of a limp. One leg was a little bit shorter than the other.

We were burning kerosene lamps and living out in the country. And pumpin' water out of the well. Anyway, he saw we were just poor country folks. I think that encouraged him more than anything else, because he saw I wasn't used to any luxuries. He proposed the first time he came. He was sixty-four and he never had been married, but he was intent on doin' it just right. And so he asked Dad for me. I was forty-nine years old. And I remember what Dad told him. He said, "Well, she's old enough to make up her own mind."

I remember I was trying to teach science at a high school, and it was just at the beginning of World War II. And all the scientists had been drafted or had volunteered. I didn't know enough about science to teach the stuff, and my pupils knew it, too. And I thought, when he proposed, that anything would beat trying to teach science, and so I didn't say "no."

Later I asked him why it was that it took so long to get interested in me. And he said, "Well, I thought you were just a career woman." That was the last kind of woman he wanted.

The only good thing about working for the state was he didn't have to retire when he got retirement age; he worked until he was eighty-eight. He didn't worry the least bit about being paid seventy-five dollars a month because he had me to see that we never wanted for food. I bought a home where I'd have a garden, four good apple trees, too. And I also had room to raise chickens in the back. It's gone now. Urban renewal took it.

Dr. Harper was a collector—they never do throw anything away. I was a bad housekeeper when I lived with him, 'cause he wouldn't let me throw anything away. He took pictures, thousands and thousands of pictures, which he developed himself the old-fashioned way in a darkroom. He had taken about six thousand pictures of architecture and had his pictures classified.

He had also taken thousands and thousands of cemetery records. That was unusual. Not many people would have been interested in that. But by taking down the names of people and the dates—from the stones, you know, he could tell about epidemics, about the different diseases that swept through the area.

He had fifteen hundred railroad timetables that he had collected. The old railroads are gone.

Do the timetables still exist?

Yes. At the University of Iowa. He was fifteen years older than I was and expected to die before I did. He said, "I'm giving you these timetables because they're worth something—about as much as an insurance policy." He made out a one-sentence will, and I had it duly witnessed and notarized. And he said, "I hereby bequeath all my property, such as it is, to my first, only, and beloved wife." He died at eighty-eight.

Theirs was indeed a wonderful marriage. They were wed on the twenty-third of the month, and for twenty-three years thereafter, Dr. Harper never failed to celebrate the twenty-third of each month. As Mary Harper confided, *He called it our "monthiversary."*

The conversation about Dr. Harper prompts a final reminiscence in which the juxtaposition is made of two traditional Southern folk customs, Sacred Harp and decoration day. The first is a form of religious folk music. It can be traced from medieval England and then to New England, but it has taken firm roots especially in the Southeast, including Georgia, where many have worked on songbooks to keep it alive since the early settlement days. The notes are shaped and the nomenclature is customarily sung prior to the lyrics.

The unique sound of Sacred Harp, of "fa-sol-la" singing, derives in the main from the four-part harmony of mixed voices—men or women alike being permitted to take any of the parts.

The second is a springtime custom in the South. Members of countless communities set aside a special day to visit the old, untended—often small and rural—cemeteries and do together whatever needs to be done in the way of cleaning up. Grass is cut; overgrowth trimmed; grave markers secured and cleaned; and flowers are brought and planted. It's a sociable time for all the Good Samaritans who come to visit as well as to work. Decoration day and Sacred Harp singings have much in common, including "dinner on the ground" and the presence of dedicated folks ranging in age from toddlers to great grandparents.

I can remember when they had the Sacred Harp singing and when they changed from the four [Sacred Harp shape] notes to seven [Christian Harmony shape] notes. And they called them the new books and the old books. My dad could go up and down the line in front of the audience singing all those fa-sol-la notes first, without looking at the book.

We used to have a big cemetery at Russ Chapel—that's where I went to Sunday School. Sometimes a grave'd sink down, you know, after people had been buried long enough for the casket to rot out and cave in. They always had an annual decoration day, and they always fixed the graves by puttin' sand on 'em. They made little pointed mounds like this [placing her finger tips together to indicate the shape].

Well, my dad was always humming, and he used to sit in the front door. And he'd sing:

> *When I was sinking down,*
> *Sinking down, sinking down,*
> *When I was sinking down,*
> *O my soul, O my soul!*

That's one song I didn't like that was a fa-sol-la. Dad would sing this song after dark, sitting in the door. And I was thinking about those graves that were sinking down. And I didn't want my dad to be sinking down. So I didn't like for him to be singing that at all.

I'm still homesick when I hear mixed voices singing and somebody leading the singing.

Now you see what can happen if you pick up your phone and dial your grandmother (or grandfather or Aunt Tillie or Uncle Bob—or local nursing home or day care center for the elderly) and say: "Grandma, I've taken up collecting folklore—you know, traditions and customs and songs and the like—and I'd be so pleased if you'd let me come over tomorrow or next week, and bring my tape recorder, while you tell me about some of the old times. Do you think we might (around here, we say "might could") do that?"

Just you wait.

Managing A Growing Collection

Once you got the hang of it, you discovered how easy it is to manage a growing collection of cards and papers in your folklore file. In the same way, you can expect a fruitful harvest of tapes and photographs to yield unlimited enjoyment in return for a minimal investment of time.

Transcribing tapes, a procedure considered mandatory in archives, is tedious, exacting work. If you should ever donate your tapes to an archive or special collection, the institution that receives them will have the facilities to make transcriptions. In the meanwhile, assuming that you will eventually have quite a few taped interviews in your folklore collection, you should have a relatively painless way of keeping it "inventoried."

An inventory serves in lieu of a written transcript as a convenient table of contents to a taped interview.

Below the identifying *who, what, when, where,* and *by whom,* you might draw a vertical line down the rest of the page, so that you will have two unequal columns. The one on the left should be no more than two inches in width. As you play back an interview, you will be filling out the right-hand column by making a sort of laundry list of the subjects covered in conversation.

You might literally make a list, or, if you prefer, write your inventory in short essay form. Just remember that it is your collection to enjoy and to organize your own way.

The left-hand column is for listing any details which are related to the interview but are not a direct part of its contents. Extraneous sounds, for instance, should be identified alongside the topics of conversation which correspond with their occurrence. Even if, at a time much later, you were able to recall what these are, anyone listening to your tapes but unfamiliar with the circumstances of the interview itself would certainly wonder about them.

So, note such sounds on the tape as clocks chiming, doors slamming, cars driving by, another person entering the room, and so on. The same column should also be used to cite the presence of accompanying materials (perhaps stored separately), like photographs or slides.

Such an inventory serves at least two important purposes. One is immediate. When you want to listen to a particular section on a tape, you won't ever have to locate it by random searching.

If, for example, you wanted to find Mrs. Harper's version of the doodle bug rhyme in order to compare it with another you've collected more recently, you would simply go to the folder in which you keep your inventories and look under *H* for Harper. A glance at each of the contents of her interview sheets would soon produce the information that the rhyme in question is recited just before the final item on Side 3 of a C90. You can then quickly fast-forward or rewind the proper cassette to the desired spot.

Inventories also serve an ultimate purpose. They amount to an act of kindness second only to having collected the recorded information in the first place. Loved one or library, whichever the repository for your taped collection a long time from now, your name will be twice blessed because you cared enough to keep your gift or legacy so well catalogued.

Here is a sample inventory sheet, which may serve as a model from which to devise your own:

Interviewer's name and complete address:_____

Interviewee's name and address: _____

Exact location of interview: _____
(e.g., kitchen or, e.g., room number of nursing home)

Date of interview:_____
(This could be the third in a series of interviews with one individual.)

Equipment used:_____
(Identify the tape recorder by brand and model no.)

(Either) Tape:_____
(If reel to reel, identify brand, size, and speed.

(Or) Cassette:_____
(Identify brand and amount of recording time, e.g., C-90.)

Amount of tape used per side:_____
(e.g., Side 3, all; Side 4, about half. Sides 1 and 2 would have been previously inventoried.)

Side 3: Early childhood in Sand Mountain
  Childhood roaming
    Following Grandpa with the traps
  Dad trapping quail in snow time
  First shoes
  Christmas
    Staying awake for Santa Claus
    How the Oranges spoiled one Christmas
  Uncle Alfred
  First day of school
  Tree stump recitations

Background conversation between Mrs. Harper's roommate and her daughter. Begins here and continues intermittently throughout interview.

  Hair
    Anecdote about lice
    Having picture made after haircut
    Opinions on artificially whitened hair
  Growing sweet potatoes
  Picking blackberries
  Lost in the swamp
  Wet weather wash place
  Fears
    Booger man
    Running away from Dad and the rock incident
    Dug wells
    Typhoid
    Water witching
    Blasting wells
  Bears:Dad and Grandpa
    Mary and Ruth: "Scare Me Again"
  Childhood games
    "Grandma Hobblegobble"
    "Acme" or "Atme Over"
    "Shadows"

The snapshots of Mrs. Harper making the appropriate gestures. (You will have labeled the envelope of photos to correspond to the label on the tape.)

    Tops
    "Pretty Bird in My Cup"
    "In and out the Window"
  Mother Goose
    Nipping noses
  Song about homesickness
  Jump ropes from cross vines
    Smoking cross vines

Recorder turned off for a few minutes while attendant came to see about Mrs. Harper.

  Collecting arrowheads
  Mill dam song
  Doodle bug rhyme
  Cob dolls
End of Side 3.

Side 4: (Then proceed to note its contents in much the same way as for Side 3. Use a second page if necessary.)

Harvesting Grass Roots:
On The Other Side Of The Fence

On-the-Go Collecting

So, where do you go to collect after you've interviewed your grandmother—and perhaps your whole family? "Grandmother," remember, serves as a code word for someone close to you, with whom you can communicate easily, and who is willing to relate her traditions. What else can you collect once you've begun to mine your own memory and those of the folks closest to you? And how else do you go about it?

In brief, you harvest folklore in your community at large. For urban, small town, or rural collectors alike, all it takes is good information in order to extend your grassroots harvesting from yourself and your immediate family into your own neighborhood, then into the community; and that information is very easy to come by.

Finding Your Sources—At Home and Away

More than you might anticipate, once you start making out collection cards and doing your first stint of interviewing, people catching wind of your new pastime will offer you leads. By word of mouth alone, you'll obtain more leads to folks who perform traditional arts, carry on particular folk skills, or collect artifacts themselves than you'll be able to follow up.

So, here's a new use to which you can put those 4" x 6" cards: Maintain a resource file for yourself. Every time someone tells you about a grave site where a legendary Gypsy king is buried, or gives you directions to the remains of a century-old church with hand-crafted pews; every time you learn of a fiddle maker who lives in your community, or a man who makes grandfather clocks, or a group in town that meets regularly to clog dance, take down all the available information on a handy 4" x 6" card. Take down the name of the artist, craftsperson, owner, or person in charge; note the address, or as precise an idea of location as your informant is able to supply, the phone number, or at least the full name of the resource person so that you can find the number in a phone directory.

Organize your resource file by topics, labeling dividers: "Dancers," "Musicians," "Traditional Craftspersons," and the like. Then alphabetize the resource names under such topic headings. On each card include also the source of your information—the person who gave you the lead—in case you need more specific information later.

Secondly, augment your word-of-mouth resource file by becoming alert to information in local news sources—your neighborhood paper, for example, if you live in a large city—to learn of people, places, and events that appeal to the interests of a folklore collector. Not only will you come upon interesting feature stories about folks in your community whom you might wish to interview when you find the time; but you will also be informed of public events that a folklore collector would not want to miss, such as fiddlers' conventions or bluegrass festivals, trade days and fairs that feature traditional crafts or ethnic culture, even occasions for the performance of religious folk music.

By means of local radio and TV announcements as well as newspapers, you can keep informed about special events such as blues or folk music concerts and visiting folk art exhibits. Normally, you would neither wish nor be able to attend as many events as you learn about in this manner. However, keeping a calendar record of these over a period of time will allow you to become familiar with the pattern of intervals at which various civic and municipal organizations afford folk culture a chance to go public. Once into folklore collecting, you soon discover that the possibilities for collecting folklore away from home are as unlimited as those for travel itself.

Whether you plan your vacation to accommodate your folklore collecting or wish to collect during free time when you happen to be traveling for another reason, you're bound to enjoy exploring regional folklife down the road from your own backyard. Perhaps you will be amazed by differences between folk environments; perhaps you will be even more surprised to find yourself so quickly at home in a new backyard.

Try to anticipate future travels by taking advantage of any opportunities to get your name on long-distance mailing lists that would enable you to receive advance notices of folk festivals, fairs, and musical events taking place elsewhere in the country. Then transfer the relevant information to index cards to be placed in a special section of your resource file. In addition, it's always a good idea to check with friends, local chambers of commerce, and regional publications for suggestions about what a folklore collector might see and do on an out-of-town trip.

In your own backyard, your folklore collecting can be applied to interests and contacts you already have as easily as it can also help you develop new ones. If you're a feminist, collect women's lore. If you're active socially in cathedral, church, or synagogue (or wish to be), collect religious folklore—the traditions which are not part of written Scripture or doctrine but which circulate informally in regionally and socially defined religious folk groups.

Some folks make a specialty of collecting graffiti. There's always some around, no matter where you do your circulating. As ancient a folk tradition as man's early cave drawings, it is as honest a reflection of the folk mind as anonymity will allow. Despite such formidable enemies as the paintbrush and scouring pad, graffiti persists as the free press of the folk.

It might be fun to investigate whether types and topics of wall writings (See the Appendix for some classification headings) vary predictably with their locations. In that case it helps to collect with a member of the opposite sex. Wall-scribbled witticisms may be without socially redeeming qualities, but they are never without socially revealing qualities. If you enjoy trying to figure out human beings, graffiti will give you endless food for thought about attitudes and emotional needs.

Specialist or generalist—whether you end up collecting whatever folklore happens to cross your path, or whether you become hooked on religious folk music only, dulcimer lore only, or traditional foodways only— the tips and illustrations to be presented here should offer you several approaches toward collecting from among people, places, and things.

Techniques for Collecting

One of your main reasons for getting into folklore was to get out of yourself a bit. Perhaps you think you are shy and worry about stumbling over your words when talking to strangers. You want to know how to go about interviewing for folklore from folks who are perfect strangers at first.

To this collector's way of thinking, the folks from whom the lore is obtained are the best part of being a folklorist. Learning to approach those who may be strangers at first and talking with them at ease, perhaps to develop lasting friendships, is something you can do more readily than you might think. It is the nature of folklore to be comfortably shared.

It remains, therefore, for you to get down to the nitty-gritty of becoming so well versed in the mechanics of using your tape recorder in public and in approaching folks to conduct interviews with them that you can function competently and thus confidently, no matter where your interests lead you.

Indoors or out, seated or on foot, if your cassette recorder is small enough, you can hold it in one hand during any interviewing situation, so long as you place yourself within good earshot of your interviewee (determined, remember, by testing). While recording in this manner, you can look at the tape in motion and check for the amount of taping time elapsed.

To free your hands, or if your cassette recorder is too large and heavy to be comfortably held for long periods of time, the companion tricks of wearing the mike at your shoulder and placing the connected recorder into an inexpensive, lightweight backpack come in very handy during interviews on the go.

You will be able to operate the recorder in the backpack quite comfortably by using the "on-off" switch on the attached mike. You must remain alert to the passage of recording time, however, so as not to neglect changing tapes promptly. You also must be sure to look at the mike switch as you operate it to avoid losing an interview by assuming incorrectly that you know "on" from "off" through your fingertips.

Equipped with a compact recorder with condenser mike, or backpacked machine with mike worn like a boutonniere or corsage, you'll be set to follow a demonstrator about or walk alongside an informant—whether you're at a folk festival, attending a "trade day," out in a planted field, near a mule-drawn sorghum mill, or strolling the grounds of an auditorium or rural home—and keep right on recording.

In or out of sight, the tape recorder must never be used surreptitiously. Legalities aside, it is simply unethical to invade anyone's privacy by tape recording them without their knowledge as well as their consent. This fundamental principle should cause you no frustration in your folklore-gathering efforts. Very few people are ever likely to refuse their permission—providing that it is requested considerately and, of course, that their performances or verbal accounts are recorded openly.

One of the reasons that a public site or event is such a good place to begin collecting folklore in your community is that the resource people you would want to contact are there in order to communicate with the public. The folklore collector has no reason to intrude on anyone's privacy or to attempt to win over a recalcitrant source—not with so many folks willing to give you permission to record and shoot pictures and to give you all the time and help they can.

If by any chance you foresee publishing all or part of any interview, you will need to obtain specific permission to do so from your informants—preferably in writing. But since, as a folklore collector, you automatically make a record of the name and address of anyone who grants you an interview, you can always write or revisit an informant (or his heirs if need be) should you seek such permission long after an interview has taken place.

Having placed yourself in a setting open to the public, you should have no problem approaching a potential informant. Just walk right up to the person you would like to talk to. Smile. Say, "Hello, I'm _____ _____ (first, last name)." Initiate a warm handshake, and continue, "I collect folklore, and I'm very interested in _____" (whatever prompted you to approach that person in the first place).

If you're in a gathering place which is frequented by regulars, who thus constitute a folk group (the site could be a "deli," tavern, coffeehouse, farmer's market, or reading room), it won't be long before you're doing an actual interview with the tape recorder going—either then and there, or by having arranged to meet again at the same spot. The stated subject or purpose of the interview could be your fascination with the very place you're in, as a folk group hangout. The interviewee to whom you said hello might be a proprietor, manager, or a visitor like you.

The setting could also be a park, auditorium, or shopping center on a special occasion—some sort of folklife event, perhaps a festival, performance, demonstration, or exhibition. Many types of gatherings fall into these categories, from block parties to heritage celebrations to fiddlers' conventions to arts and crafts shows.

Either way, the experience belongs to the social folklife of a community. You're not an intruder. In the latter situation, you are part of a crowd where quite a few of the folks around you are interested in much the same things as you; they just haven't all made up their minds to be folklore collectors yet. You, however, have discovered someone you would like to interview. How do you justify approaching that person?

With tape recorder in hand or backpack, with camera strap slung over your shoulder, you are already communicating a silent message. Though non-explicit, it precludes your being perceived as frivolous. Keep in mind several factors:

You're quite safe from having your intentions mistaken. This is a public event intended to enlighten folks on folklife. The performer, demonstrator, or exhibitor whom you approach wouldn't be there unless he or she were trying to get people interested in the very thing you want to talk about.

There may be quite a crowd, but you need not feel apologetic about monopolizing the time of a demonstrator or performer. In that crowd will be a number of people for whom you're doing a favor. They're just as interested as you are, but they're too shy to ask the resource person any questions. Whatever he or she tells and shows you, they are going to hear and see as well.

You may be shy yourself, but you're not going to be the center of attention. Those who are listening in on your interview will focus their attention on the person who is making an extra effort to put on a good demonstration.

Once you've broken the ice, you'll find that bystanders will speak up and ask their questions during your interview. That may well put bonus information on your tape.

To obtain the best results, have a checklist on hand, but follow the dictates of your own spontaneous curiosity. Keep everything informal. A great deal of the information you're after will be forthcoming as a matter of course. So don't worry about the structure of an interview, the sequence of your questions.

By giving your informants room to talk themselves out, you will only have to consult your checklist and organize a few questions at the end, which account for just those details not yet supplied in the course of demonstration or conversation.

Regrettably, most of us are guilty of missing opportunities to increase our knowledge for fear of being accused of asking a stupid question. What's really stupid is our fear. As a folklore collector, *never* be afraid to show your ignorance. Your purpose is to obtain information. Who would want to do a lot of heavy explaining to a know-it-all?

Indeed, when an informant asks whether you're familiar with a certain process, event, or term, if you were to say, "Yes" (unless you could honestly say, "No") you might close off further discussion. Therefore, develop the habit of replying neutrally, "Tell me about it." Never make a point of demonstrating superior knowledge—if you are blessed with such. The less you assume you already know about a subject, the more you are going to learn from an informant.

Nor is there any point in trying to prove how many questions you are capable of coming up with—unless you'd rather hear yourself talk than the informant. The less talking and the more listening you do, the better your interviews will be.

The sincerity of your interest, the depth of your curiosity, the respect you indicate by giving an interviewee your full attention—these are what count, not how much you do or do not already know about an informant's area of expertise.

It is often said that an interviewer should be very careful not to ask "yes-no" questions but formulate "information" questions instead. It's the difference between inquiring, "Do you like your work?" and asking, "How do you feel about working so hard to write a song?" The first query might lead to the one-word response, while the second is more apt to produce fifteen minutes of nonstop revelations.

The suggestion is a good one, though it takes much time and patience to master. But ask yourself what would be so bad if, for one moment of relaxed abandonment, you forgot and asked, "Do you like your work?" only to hear, "Yes sir," followed by—perish the thought—silence. There is no reason you can't recoup at once merely by saying, "What I really meant to ask was, 'How do you feel about putting so much hard work into composing a song?'"

On the basis of another much-touted conventional belief, an interviewee should be steered away from the pursuit of tangents. However, to always maneuver one's informants into sticking to just one subject at a time is to risk missing some mighty good folklore. It is often better to give an informant his lead; it's surprising how much bonus information an interviewer can pick up that way.

So please, no anxiety attacks about your skills as an interviewer. Nobody, least of all your willing informant, is going to pressure you into proving your competence as a slick professional. Forget about yourself. Concentrate on the person who is having a fine time showing and telling you things of importance to you both. If one set of words fails to express what you intend, try another. There's no substitute for genuine interest. Once you have that, you're more than halfway home.

Artifacts and Craftspersons

Predominantly utilitarian objects are usually associated with crafts; creative ones, with arts. But because yesterday's functional item can become tomorrow's art object, and since we often say "art" in appreciation of a high degree of skill, distinctions between arts and crafts can become quite fuzzy. If your purposes of classification in folklore collecting require clear distinctions, consistency in applying both terms should suffice.

Many of the same situations in which you find yourself harvesting traditional sayings, beliefs, and customs will provide occasions for you to acquire material artifacts. In this respect, again, you can build as specialized or diversified a collection as initiative, opportunity, your pocketbook, or even your imagination will allow. For there are several ways to go about this very pleasant part of folklore collecting.

Collecting Folk Artifacts

Removed from its context, the folk object gives pleasure as a symbol of the folk culture from which it derives. Folk artifacts can be primary—the object itself—or secondary—a representation of a folk expression or object.

Even if you can afford to collect folk objects of art, to decorate your home with them, to make gifts of them, but especially if you can't afford to do much of that, you might enjoy some of the creative aspects of collecting the secondary folk artifact.

For instance, you might carry around an autograph book, the kind that you used to have in school. Get your friends to contribute the same kinds of inscriptions they once exchanged in autograph or class yearbooks. Ask children to sign it, too, so that your collection will include contemporary variants. In time, you will have accumulated a highly prized collector's item.

Collect handed-down recipes, not the kind that are clipped from printed sources, but those that circulate traditionally within a family and are attributed to a grandmother or earlier ancestor. Try to include traditional recipes from members of ethnic groups, too. And just as you would for other collected verbal or customary lore, record all the situational details you can learn about the preparation of each dish. Turn this special collection into a homemade, perhaps hand-lettered, cookbook, and you'll have another treasured artifact. (Copies run off on a duplicating machine would make wonderful gifts.)

Epitaph rubbings are another form of creative collecting. Making them can be a pleasant hobby that combines weekend outings (often down country roads) with a love of history and a certain amount of craftsmanship on your part. For rubbings require a good eye, patience, and a sense of composition.

Cemeteries are quite lovely, peaceful places. Choose sites which appear most indigenous to community life and least reflective of the funeral home industry, though. Traditional markers will tell you a great deal about community and personal life (not death), human attitudes and values, and homemade creativity in verse.

On a 4" x 6" card to accompany each rubbing, give the name and location of the cemetery where the informant data usually goes. Slides, while no substitute for the satisfaction of doing rubbings, would augment the documentation, for some grave markers can only be photographed: those that have small shelters constructed over them; those with ceramic-glazed photographs of the deceased; or markers that are carvings of angel's heads and wings, or wooden silhouettes of human figures, or even death masks. Once in a rare while, you might discover a burial site with a brightly painted picket fence around it and real toys, placed there by survivors of a much-remembered child.

Now, to make epitaph rubbings, you will need some sturdy art paper, preferably in rolls in order to cut large sheets to specification. Some people like to use rice paper, but you may find it too flimsy as well as slippery. Chalk or charcoal tends to smudge easily and to flake off the paper, especially after a rubbing has been in storage for some time. A rubbing wax "heel ball" is the ideal marking agent; but if it is difficult to obtain, try an art supply store for very thick crayons—wide enough to be used broadside.

Bring along a brush or whisk broom so that you can clear away any debris that prevents the paper from lying flat against a headstone. Cut or tear off a sheet of paper long enough to cover the entire grave marker the text and design of which you wish to reproduce. Position the paper against the stone. Holding this paper steady is the hardest part. It helps considerably to have someone with you. But if no extra hands are available, use masking tape or any other means of affixing the paper to the stone without tearing the sheet or leaving traces of adhesive behind.

As soon as the paper is secured over the tombstone, hold your chunky crayon parallel to the surface (or use the wax heel ball), and rub it as evenly as you can over the entire area. The engraving will show up white against a dark background to render an actual-size reproduction of the headstone.

There is no cause for concern that your newfound hobby might be considered disrespectful; on the contrary, in England, where brass rubbings are especially prized, it is a traditional pastime.

Store rubbings carefully in oversized folders. Since these are quite expensive to purchase, you might prefer to exercise your ingenuity and make them or get a stationery store to save for you the empty containers that poster boards come in. But you might be so taken with some of the rubbings you produce that you'll hang them on your walls.

Primary artifacts—works of folk art and handcrafted examples of material culture—make wonderful gifts for friends as a refreshing alternative to the store-bought object. But it takes the fun as well as the purpose out of collecting to confuse folk artifacts with "merchandise." Trade days, crafts fairs, and folk festivals are legitimately the "department stores" of the collector-buyer, but only in a limited sense.

Purchase directly from the artist or craftsperson, for a genuine folk artist usually cares less about making a profit than about making an object and will not mind your lingering without necessarily buying. Indeed, you can count on a mutual understanding that there is no direct correlation between what a person can afford to buy and what a person can afford time to learn about and appreciate.

Be selective when you do buy folk artifacts. Shopping comparatively means spending time with the artists, talking to them, learning about their work and the pride they take in it, until you know which potter's wares, which quilter's "Log Cabin," which instrument maker's dulcimer will mean the most to you. Often a collector-informant relationship initiated at a public event can be advantageously followed up. Once you have identified traditional quilters, shingle makers, wood carvers, or toy crafters in your resource file, you can go directly to their studios or workshops—often at their homes—and purchase from stock, place special orders, or even trade for items.

But you can also collect color slides of primary objects—quilts or wooden Indians or split-rail fences—labelled as to their maker, when they were crafted, and the names attributed to any patterns or to the processes. And you can record anecdotes, explanatory comments, or any history accompanying the display of a folk object or demonstration of a traditional process.

Interviewing the Craftsperson

Don't overlook the opportunities which shopping for artifacts gives the true collector to document the creative processes that go into the making of a folk object. Don't just buy a white oak split cotton basket from a traditional craftsperson; watch the basket being made. Shoot slides of each stage of the process. Ask questions about everything that comes to mind, from where the best white oaks are to be found, to what time of year is best for their harvest, to how the craftsperson learned to weave baskets, to what the names of the tools are (though nothing more complex than a pocket knife may be used after the wood has been split into bolts by means of a froe and mall).

Don't just watch the chair bottom weaver go over three, under two (or whatever the pattern may be); find out how he or she feels about doing this kind of work. Observe to learn whether the craftsperson thinks of himself or herself as an artist. Is the work a source of satisfaction? In what ways? How long has a handwoven chair bottom been known to last? How are the wooden splits or twisted ropes made out of fertilizer bag liners (or whatever the woven material) added on? What keeps the splits pliable? Ask whatever comes to mind.

Ultimately, you will want an interview or series of interviews about a given folk art, craft, or skill to include its performance or demonstration and to cover most of these areas of information:

A. About the art, craft, or skill
    1. Where it was learned
    2. When it was learned
    3. How it was learned (from whom, the circumstances)
    4. How long or regularly this practitioner has been at it
    5. The best conditions for practicing all or some of the steps
    6. The steps in the process, including variations
    7. Tools or equipment considered essential
    8. Any special terms used to describe steps in the process
B. About the artifact, product, or performance
    1. Essential content or structure
    2. Uses or applications (which are not necessarily immediately obvious)
    3. In what ways, if any, it is made or used differently today than in former times
    4. What innovations the artisan or performer has consciously introduced
    5. Whom else the artisan knows who performs a similar skill
    6. Various names for it (or its components) known to its maker
C. About the artisan or performer
    1. Birthplace
    2. Parents' occupations
    3. Number of brothers and/or sisters and order of birth

4. Region of current residence
5. How he or she makes a living
6. Age
7. Family: marital status, number of children, grandchildren, etc.
8. Implied and/or explicitly stated attitudes toward own performance or skill
9. Personality features
10. Manner of expression

Much of your pleasure in acquiring a traditionally handcrafted folk artifact—whether you buy it outright or enjoy it as one does the flowers one leaves in the garden uncut—comes from knowing as much as possible about the circumstances under which it was made. The true collector becomes familiar with both the personality of its maker and the skills involved in the making, with both the history of the art itself and the community context in which a particular performance of a traditional skill occurs.

"It Started Off Because I Like To Whittle"

Excerpts from three informal interviews taped with master craftspersons should help you know what to expect when you conduct your own. For these responsive informants, love and need are one.

Homer Ledford from Winchester, Kentucky, one of the finest folk instrument makers in the country, has made over four thousand dulcimers alone. Each bears his hallmark, a dogwood so often carved freehand "on the back end" that Homer worries lest his practiced hand makes them seem stamped out.

Homer became interested in dulcimers in 1946 while attending the John Campbell Folk School in North Carolina—an informal school that teaches traditional carving as well as folk dance and other recreational folklore.

Colista Ledford, Homer's sunny wife, tells you, *And now Homer's going to teach a course at John C. Campbell in how to*

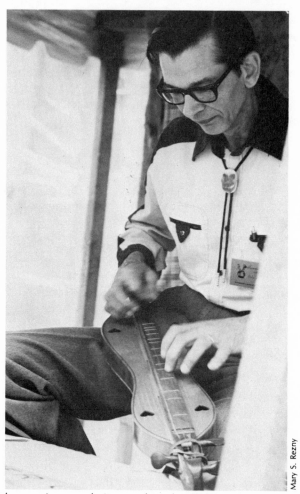

Mary S. Rezny

"All four of those strings are being used as drones. But if you tune these two strings two octaves apart, you can play melody on it." That Homer does famously, making it look quite easy to play a lively "Wildwood Flower" using a pick.

build a dulcimer. He's gonna start 'em from the raw wood up to the finished product.

Homer was born and raised in Tennessee—in the deep mountains of Tennessee; just like the east Kentucky mountains. You have to know where it is to find it.

She's from up in Paintsville, Homer points out. *I've found me a good woman—good mountain woman, you know. She's taken care of me pretty well,* Homer admits.

As far as Homer can determine, the late Jethro Amburgy and he were the first people in the nation ever to make mountain dulcimers for sale. *One time this boy in the Berea College dormitory where I lived wrote a story on me and took my picture. And lo and behold, when this came out in the* Courier Journal *Sunday Magazine, there was Jethro's picture with the story right along beside mine—two pictures: Homer and Jethro!*

Today, Homer makes instruments for customers from all over the country—mountain dulcimers mostly. But one of his proudest achievements is his invention of a new instrument, the dulcitar. The heart-shaped dulcitar seems to combine the best features of each instrument in the synthesis: the sweet sound of the dulcimer but the resonance of the guitar. Moreover the six nylon strings and five chromatic frets allow the instrument to be played in any key, just like a guitar, while the remaining frets, which are "diatonic up the scale," permit the instrument to be played like a dulcimer, with open chord tuning.

Homer was innovative in his dulcimer craft right from the start: *I didn't think much of the three strings on it. Traditionally, most of them have three strings, but we have four and five on ours. My biggest know-how, as far as making them today, is what I learned on my own, because many of them weren't fretted right. And nearly every one that I had seen had been coming apart. They didn't have good glues, or didn't know where to get good glues. Some were nailed together—literally!*

Glue won't penetrate rosewood because it has a natural oil in it. You do need to reinforce your joints on rosewood. But black walnut does beautifully, so we don't have to reinforce most of them.

Ledford dulcimers should be seen from the back as well as front: *Now this is an inlay. This back is two pieces. In other words, this piece was sawed from that piece so that you have a "book match," we call it—like opening up a book. So the grain matches this side—the streaks, roughly the same.* He lays the

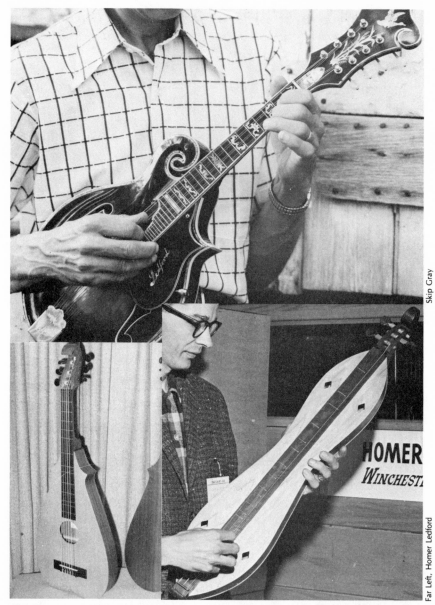

Skip Gray

Far Left, Homer Ledford

Three instruments handcrafted by Homer Ledford of Winchester, Kentucky: top, a Gibson F style mandolin; bottom left, dulcitar (his own invention); bottom right, a dulcimer.

instrument across his lap and plays "Aunt Rhody" and a version of "Soldier's Joy," ending with "shave and a hair cut; two bits."

I start with a rough board, smooth one side, and for the back and top I run it through the table saw. You have to have a basic table saw and a band saw and it helps to have a joiner, drill press, and a sander. I don't have any automatic equipment whatsoever. But, after twenty years of twisting around making these pegs, I've got this little thing I made—a little motor with the speed slowed down, with a slot—turns real slow. I put the peg head in that and out over the trimmer, so I don't have to twist my wrist so much—I have some arthritis. It twists for me, but I have to guide it. But it's fun. Feel like I'm beating the system.

Back in the mountains, the way they did it, they probably sat down by the fire in the wintertime or a rainy day instead of going fishing, and they'd whittle it out. They'd take a chisel fashioned from a file, and dig out the interior where the strings go down in there.

Homer Ledford's dulcimers are traditional in size and shape. His major innovation is to have widened the fretboard by half an inch; the fingerboard by one-fourth inch. Homer recommends replacing the strings *every three months regardless, although some folks insist on replacing them every three years regardless!*

Besides his sense of humor (he kids about his being so skinny that when he turns sideways, he's invisible), and his ingratiating smile (untouched by perfectionistic orthodontistry), Homer Ledford's most winning quality is the wonder in his own voice when he finds himself telling you:

You know, my hobby is my work! It started off because I liked to whittle. And I've done a lot of whittling on my thumb, but I still like to whittle, I do. But it's not so much the making now; it's the playing. We do have a bluegrass band, and I have fun with that now. We're just kind of knocking around a little; it's not professional, especially.

Ed and Pansy Cress both like to whittle, too—life-size wooden Indians. You admire an entire family of them: man, woman, and child. The three figures represent months of work. *Actually, anybody can do it,* says Pansy Cress. Carving a life size family of wooden Indians is no big deal to this grandmother of thirty, who thinks nothing of putting up all fifty of her clan when they all come home overnight.

One winter when Ed became ill, Pansy finished a carving for him. That's how they became a team:

We just drifted into this after Ed retired from the sawmill, the coal mines, and all like that. At first, we kind of block out the

Now that Ed Cress has lost most of his sight his sensitive fingers guide his carving knife. The latter is so sharp "it'll stick to the wood," or shave the hair off his arm quicker than you can blink in astonishment.

chief with a chain saw. That takes a lot of the old, big wood away. And after that, we use chisels and hammers, and get around the arms and the face and back of the feathers, and so like that. And then we come to the knife stage, you know, there you use the little hand tools. And then, after sanding, we use clear wood sealer.

The wood is buckeye. Some folks call it horse chestnut, but they tell me it's not the same thing. Here it grows along rivers and creeks. We have people who work in the timber, and they save us the good pieces.

Just ask Ed Cress, who is whittling an owl, how sharp his knife has to be. He demonstrates by shaving a spot on his arm bald as a melon with one quick stroke of his whittling knife:

A knife needs to do that. You don't need a dull knife. It'll slip and cut your fingers off. But if it's sharp, it'll stick to the wood.

Ed's from Somerset. He got interested in whittling at work. *I've worked in sawmills, coal mines, farming, you name it. I suppose I enjoyed coal mining more than anything. That's how I happened to be carving. The last work I did was loading coal in barges.* He'd whittle while he waited for a barge to return for reloading. He'd whittle while watching over machinery.

You've been wondering about that strange mark in the wood, right in the center of the statue of the Indian woman. Ed laughs and explains:

It's a knot of wood. It was an accident, too. In growing up, a tree, when it's not very tall yet, will have several branches coming out. But a lot of times the little branches die and drop off the tree. And the trunk grows over and covers it up. That leaves a swelled place, not a knot showing on the outside. So when we cut into the tree, there it was. There the knot was. And it just came out in the right place for a belly button!

Pansy, surveying all their carvings, calls over, *This is good for us. It's good for older people. Almost everything that's made here is made from nothing, you might say: Go out and get an old big log and make something. Actually, anybody can do it. We learn through need.*

"I used to fix them for artificial fruit and stuff. But then meeting and talking with a lot of people, who wanted to make their bread in it like the old-timey people, I stopped staining and finishing them. Now I just rub them down with cooking oil, and people go make bread in them, and that's that."

Ed tells you about his friend *William McClure* from Mt. Vernon who likes to do his whittling with a chain saw and sometimes with a froe. Bill (who's got Ed beat by a head, since his children number a baker's dozen) makes dough bowls:

I do quite a bit of dough trays with a chain saw. Before that I was strictly into farming. I'm from Rock Castle County right down between two big mountains where you have to look up to see the sun at twelve.

I have my timber ten to twelve feet long out to there. I mark all my trees and saw the insides out first. I saw so many strips down longways with the tree and then go crossways. Then I just take a hammer and knock all the little squares out. If you lay an inch board down there, and set your bar on the inch board, and then mark the top of your tray and stick you a piece of tape there, and saw to your tape, you know where you're going.

Dough trays, or dough bowls, have traditionally been used for kneading dough in breadmaking. Is that what people use them for nowadays? Bill guesses so.

A lady from California that was on my place about three months ago claims she makes her light bread in one all the time. She wanted me to saw her one three feet long and just as wide as I could get it. She wanted to make up a lot of bread at once.

Bill is also skilled in making traditional wooden shingles for folk houses and out buildings:

In selecting a good tree to make shingles from, you look at the bark of the tree. You've got to have a good straight-grain bark tree.

This froe has been in my family as long as I can remember. I wouldn't have any idea how old it is. I'm fifty-six and it's older.

There's quite a bit of difference in working against the grain and working with the grain. If your timber is big enough, you bust it down into eighths—wedges like a pie. This is the heart wood, which you can't use in the shingles. Then you go across the grain and bring your knees out and break this down from the center, to make four bolts. Then you make four shingles from each bolt. The heartwood is firewood, which is about all you can do about it.

Bill deviates in his procedure from other shingle makers you've talked to elsewhere in that he avoids shaving his shingles with a drawing knife. Softspoken, he is nonetheless very insistent that the shingles will be much more waterproof, and therefore longer lasting, if they are left as they are: *Anytime that you cut these grains here, you see, then that opens the pores and lets in the water.*

A young bearded fellow mentions to Bill that the shingles on his new roof curled up when he tried to lay them on the new of the moon. They commiserate over it. Here's Bill's end of the discussion:

You can take two pieces from the same piece of wood and lay one down on the new of the moon, and it'll turn up on each end

Bill McClure demonstrates shingle splitting: "Any kind of red oak makes good shingles, as long as it is free from limbs and knots." (As Ed Cress's Indian statue with the belly button is not. Bill, who knows all about it, still laughs at that). "But I will say one thing, white oak is the best."

like a rocking chair. Lay the other one down on the old of the moon, and it'll lay right flat and go right down on the ground.

There's so many people that don't seem to believe in that. I'll tell you what made me a strong believer of it. When I was twelve years old and my father was building a curing tobacco barn, he used to put the shingles on, and I was standing there handing them to him. Three or four courses right up next to the top on the last side—we was finishing on out so we could house tobacco—I remember him saying: "Maybe these won't last no time." So I asked why, like any other person would. He said: "We're putting them on at the new of the moon."

And I'm a-tellin' you, two or three years after that, them things just turned up and got just as raggedy as they could be,

Mary S. Rezny

Edna Ritchie Baker proudly displays cornshuck dolls, a Ritchie family tradition carried on by seven of the women in this well-known Kentucky mountains clan: "It all started with our oldest sister May, who is eighty now. She used to make rag dolls when she was little. She'd take a piece of cotton and roll it up in a circle, and then tie the top and pull it down and tie the neck. That's the way most of our cornshuck dolls are different; most people don't put necks on them. May has made thousands and thousands." Though each of the seven sisters has her own way of making them, all the dolls, their sweet faces simply drawn in fine point pen, are collectively known for their unmistakable Ritchie look.

Mary S. Rezny

Sarah Bailey of Bledsoe, Kentucky, teaches others so that they can send their children to school with the money earned selling handicrafts. "I didn't have an education, but I do all kinds of work. I card, and spin, and weave. I make cornshuck flowers and baskets. I make cornshuck rugs." She is grace in motion at her antique spinning wheel, really a "walking wheel"—the kind that gives the spinner maximum control because the only source of tension on the fiber is that between the spinner's hand and the spindle.

*and the others just lay there just like you just put them on. They
work with nature. It's true.*

*Same thing about planting potatoes. You can plant them on
the new of the moon and you can't hardly keep them covered
up from getting sunburned. On the old of the moon, you have
to dig knee-deep to get 'em.*

Apprenticeships. An informal apprenticeship might come about as
the result of doing a series of interviews with a craftsperson. You
become so interested in the craft that you ask to be shown exactly
how it's done by having your own attempts supervised. Having
acquired their own skills in much the same informal manner,
traditional artisans will welcome your interest and are likely to be as
pleased by opportunities to coach others as you are grateful for a
chance to learn from them.

When you approach a craftsperson for instruction, come prepared. Bring a plastic bag of premoistened corn shucks to the
woman who is about to show you how to make cornhusk flowers or
dolls. Carry some fabric scraps to your informal quilting lesson.

You might do some carving on that block of wood by yourself, the
better to get specific pointers from a master woodcarver such as Ed
Cress on how to improve your technique. Try weaving a basket on
your own, the better to identify specific problems which an
experienced basket maker can help you solve when you go to visit.

If a folk musician shows you a few new guitar or banjo licks, if the
dulcimer maker from whom you buy an instrument gives you tips on
chords and fingering, if you learn some clogging steps, the best way
you can show your appreciation is to follow through and practice
what you've picked up.

Social Folk Groups

Almost everyone belongs to at least one social folk group. Though strong ties of region, occupation, or age may also determine the formation of such groups, their primary reason for being is sociability or the sharing of recreational experiences.

You can easily gather folk group lore from your current friends. However, if your motives for getting into folklore collecting include the wish to explore that greener grass on the other side of the fence, then you can certainly look forward to a bountiful harvest in the public fields of social-recreational folk groups.

Before you know it, you'll be shedding your role of outside observer and getting into the act as participant. Social folk groups accessible to the public are so easily found that you'll declare Southern-style, "If it'd been a snake, it would-a bit me!"

The Folk Hangout

Every community has its "hangouts"—those convivial places, usually designated for eating or drinking, which become a home away from home to a clientele that's really a folk group. The usual metaphor for the latter is "one big happy family." Indeed, the folks who frequent such a hangout are bound together socially by strong ties of region, occupation, or age.

Thus the neighborhood tavern; or taco place, where teenagers cluster on nonschool nights; or truck stop, echoing dialect-studded shop talk; or off-campus beer hall; or that heart-of-downtown coffee shop, where merchants on break orally compile their own *Wall Street Journal;* or a place like Louise's.

Every Friday night, Louise's home away from home teems with life and bursts into song. It's not age that unites this folk group, for you'll find folks there from two to eighty-two. Nor is it occupation, for you'll recognize housewives, nurses, seamstresses, beauticians, business owners, factory workers, farmers, college professors. Nor is it creed or a rung on the so-called socio-economic ladder that turns this crowd into one big, happy family. It's a shared love of bluegrass music.

The fact that you have to cheat and park in an adjacent hamburger hangout lot proves beyond a doubt that there isn't a seat in the place to be had. You go in anyway. No seats. You sidle up to a wall so you won't block anybody's view of the dozen musicians at the other end backing up two of their fellows in a ripping "Orange Blossom Special."

Before you even have a chance to lean, three guests at as many tables have made room for you. You settle in with a mug of hearty coffee and a slab of coconut cream pie in front of you, just in time for a resounding, soul-shaking rendition of "Glory Land" that has every voice in the place joining in and every face lit up. After you help with "Will the Circle Be Unbroken," you have a chance to look around.

The musicians are shifting positions in relation to the mike. A couple are changing instruments; two or three more sit down in the front booth to let several others replace them on the floor. A handsome woman steps forward to sing a full-throated "Peace in the Valley" solo.

It's 11 P.M., but well-behaved youngsters are listening to the music wide-awake; families of grandparents with parents and children chat quietly at their tables; one man, his chair backed against the table, faces toward the music, balancing a fiddle upright on his knees. It's in a paper sack; only the neck is showing.

Louise's husband, police sergeant Charles M. Snyder, presides jovially from the kitchen doorway. James, the corpulent cook, dances an improvised jig behind the counter—one partner, a gyrating dishcloth; the other, a youthful waitress on our side of the counter. A placid Louise, seated at a booth for six with her legs

Every Friday night, Louise's home away from home teems with life and bursts into song.

comfortably crossed and cup of coffee in hand, permits herself a half-smile.

Central to this shared experience—the easy comradeship, the cooperation of bass, fiddles, banjos, guitars, mandolins, and voices—is the nuclear force of Louise herself. It is to her, at a quieter time on another day, that you bring your tape recorder to do an interview over a cup of coffee on a slack afternoon.

Well, I had been in the food business about thirty-one years, and thought I'd just retire and stay at home.

So it hasn't been a life-long dream to have your own restaurant?

No. I was going to be a housewife and just quit work. Four or five weeks of that was OK, until I caught up on all my sleep and all the work I wanted to do around there, and watched all them soap operas I wanted to. And I was the most miserable human being in the world, because I missed all my people.

Louise, who always showed a healthy respect for her occupation, had a following of regular customers who'd select their dining spots by where she worked.

We were laying there in bed one morning, me and my husband, and the man that owned the building called me and wanted to lease me this business. I wasn't excited at all, but I told him I'd look at it. Well, I looked at it, and I looked at it, and I looked at it, and I looked at it. And I got more excited, and more excited, and more excited.

If it wasn't built as Louise's Restaurant, what was there before you took it over?

The first time it opened up, it was just a barbecue place. They went bankrupt. The second time it opened up, a barbecue place again, it didn't make it either.

Didn't it kind of worry you that the others hadn't been able to make a go of this location?

Uh-huh. I had a lot of people tell me, "Don't go there; it's jinxed." But, ah, I'm one of them more hardheaded people, you know. If I believe something will go, it'll go! Well, when I made up my mind to do it, I signed the papers one day and moved in the next.

And there wasn't a dish in here. There wasn't a cup, saucer, spoon, nothing. And so I made a list of what all I needed and drove to a neighboring state, and what I couldn't pick up I had shipped over here. I bought a lot and in a matter of three days, I had this place stocked and going.

Louise Snyder, who could have taught Tom Sawyer a thing or two.

Nobody could believe it. Everybody would look at me and say, "You really are a nice person, but I just don't believe you can make it here." I said, "Watch me!"

How did Louise succeed in business? Therein lies the tale:

I think word of mouth is the best advertising you can do. 'Course, when I first opened—being in the food business all these years—the first thing I did was put my picture in the paper 'cause everybody recognized me. "That's the lady!" "That's the lady!" "That's the lady!"

Now I see it takes time, but it wasn't going along as fast as I wanted it to. So, when me and my husband and my daughter and another employee was out here, and when we was going to eat, every one of us would sit at a different table to make people think we had guests.

I had a friend at a used car place, and I'd go and borrow five or six of his cars, and we'd switch 'em out and swap 'em out all the time. And this works without a doubt.

I'd go out the driveway and a couple of blocks down, and as soon as I'd give a signal that I was goin' to turn in, well, another car'd follow me in. So we'd do this all night. Some of us would be driving in and out, and—like a chain reaction—it would work.

Unable to contain your delight at her ingenuity, you remark that Louise could probably teach them a few things over at a business college.

See, I never did even get out of the seventh grade. My father died and I went to work. I was between twelve and thirteen, but I lied about my age so I could work. But I learned so much just dealing with the people.

But the musicians: There was four of them came here—the four originals that are still here—just looking for a place to play, and I was looking for anything that would create action.

So I told 'em, "Bring your tub"—one of them really plays a tub. Now, I'm not sure what note he plays on it; but he has a string on it, and he plays a tub.

J.B. H_____, James D_____, Ray P_____, and Hob T_____ were the first ones. And I told 'em, "Well, bring all y'all's tubs, and come on up here and play a few."

The next Friday night they came early and set up, and there was people! They just about wrecked trying to see what was going on inside.

And then they would stop and just have to come in and see what was drawing so many cars.

Last summer we would have so many people, there'd be a group playing on this side, a group playing in here, there'd be a group playing out there, and I would spread a tablecloth and serve them on the hood of those cars.

And you just feed the musicians, and that's all, right?

Yes, sometimes they would play all day and all night without *stopping, because they love it—sometimes when they have bluegrass contests, you know. J.B. is more or less their leader. We have a mother and a daughter from the University, one group coming in from sixty miles away, and Georgia Baker, who can really sing—'course, I knew Georgia before I came over here; she works as a seamstress.*

And there's a little girl—the child's grandmother is named Louise, and the grandfather plays the fiddle; they just all come from a musical family. And that child's not but two years old. See, we got a chair we slide under her, so she can get under the mike, and she'll sing like a little bird.

Usually, if the music is really good, the customers'll be so spellbound, they won't know that people's waiting to eat or anything else. First they come because they love the music and the food, then the atmosphere—the feeling they get.

We have two or three hours rush on Friday evening. But when that's over, usually me and my husband will sit down and relax and maybe eat or enjoy the music. And we never act like we get aggravated at people if they stay all night.

No matter what, we just go along with them—whatever they want on Friday nights, we want it too, because, after all, we used to sit here and maybe do three hamburgers. So now we do two or three hundred dollars and have done four or five. So I know I owe a lot to the music and the fans.

The American Dream seems alive and well and coming true for Louise Snyder.

The audience really responds to those religious songs. Everybody loves them. Some people don't even know each other; but when they get in here, they're all friends.

Active Involvement in a Folk Group

Whether the focus of interest is on barbershop harmony, sacred folk music, pickin' and grinnin', or the square dancers' "tip" and "hash," an absorbing, fun-filled, even healthful, shared experience tends to promote fast friendships. If you join a square dance club, take clogging lessons, or participate in regularly scheduled group folk music singing as collector and member both, you'll reap twice the benefits and feel twice as welcome.

Such groups are apt to be close-knit as a whole. For, in addition to a human nucleus, the uniting principle of a social folk group, as you have already discovered, is fellowship. There's plenty of that to be found in recreational folk dancing, more particularly in clogging.

This spirited heel-and-toe-tapping dance, usually performed by groups of couples, gives the initial impression of being a first cousin to square dancing and to buck or even jig dancing. If you're only a spectator, it's hard to sit still. The music that goes with it—the kind we generally think of as "hoe-down" music—turns one into a toe tapper, voluntarily or not.

You've seen clogging on country music and sometimes documentary news programming on TV, and you'd come to associate it mainly with the Carolinas, Georgia, and Tennessee—until a local news announcement heralded its presence in west Alabama. Your folklore collector's interests sufficiently aroused, you go to the YMCA every Friday night that you can, to observe as out-of-towners Lendal and Nora McCullar instruct a class of novices.

Devoted to clogging, Nora and Lendal McCullar (third and fourth from left) will drive anywhere to help an interested group get off the ground. At first even an observer can remember the slow-motion steps long enough to go home and try them in private. But by the end of the series of lessons, folks in the class are having themselves a ball doing fast-paced routines no outsider could emulate.

More vigorous than square dancing, clogging probably gets its name from the pounding of traditional work shoes on wooden flooring. Today's cloggers wear lightweight shoes with metal taps in an effort to carry on the tradition of feet producing a thunderous din, for floors are often concrete or tile, rarely plank.

Intermittently, through several weeks of lessons, you observe as couples with "two left feet" evolve into precision cloggers; and a stout woman, who joined for the exercise, turns trim. Before the session has ended, several members of the class have become devoted cloggers for the time of their lives.

After a lesson, the McCullars, their kids, and friends, like Bob Calvert—who come along for the sociability of the 150-mile round trip—usually stop off for a late supper. That's when you go along to tape some round table talk on a subject they can discuss tirelessly until well after midnight.

One night you do something you would never recommend to fellow collectors—turn on the tape recorder in the thick of whirling bluegrass to tape the group's conversation at Louise's. However, there are to be other interviews in more tranquil if not more delightful surroundings to yield a composite harvest, which just goes to show you that it can be fun to conduct an interview with a number of folks at once!

Clogging brought Nora and Lendal together only a few short years ago. Lendal's known how to clog for about ten years. He taught Nora three years ago, though she dances as if she'd been born doing it. You ask how they got started organizing their clogging group. While attending a square dancers' festival in Biloxi, Mississippi, Nora and Lendal picked up a few clogging steps, which they brought home to their own Town and Country square dancers.

Lendal: *And that's what turned us on, you might say.*
Nora: *And we decided that we was goin' to do some exhibitions, and we started practicing—mostly in old dusty basements or anywhere we could get. And we kept working until we got us up a routine.*
Lendal: *A real good square dance caller helped us work up routines—like a choreographer, you might say.*

Nora: *But you really have to have a group. You can't just have two or three people to keep going. You have to have a group to make it look good.*

No matter how much you may or may not already know about a particular subject in folklore, you should permit an interviewee to assume the role of authority. There is general agreement in the group that clog dancing is an Appalachian folk tradition. But, as with the banjo—perhaps our most American folk instrument, and the blues—perhaps our most American folk music, its earliest ethnic origins are difficult to analyze in specific detail. Speculation is fun, though.

Nora: *Well, nobody really knows where clogging comes from. In the books that we read, one from North Carolina says it has an Irish jig and Scottish dances, that it's German, and all that just mixed together with a little buck dancin' from the Indians thrown in for good measure.*
And they come to stir it all up and come out with cloggin'. Really, there's not any cloggin' here, like in the Carolinas and Georgia. That's where you're going to find most of it. They say they call a wooden shoe a clog.
Bob: *Clogging is an amalgamation of several things in the past. African people had their dances; black people have a rhythm called a hambone; the Scottish people had a jig; the Irish people had a jig.*
Interviewer: Man may have been dancing before he could speak.
Lendal: *The buck dancing is still a clog.*
Nora: *In different parts of the country, they call it different things, like the western swing.*
Interviewer: There's something called barn dancing in contrast with square dancing, and not everyone distinguishes between them the same way.
Lendal: *Barn dancing is the old-type of square dancing that used to be back whenever my father and mother was comin' up. In the old days you had a jug o' the corn squeezin's in the middle of the floor. In the last twenty years we took all the*

liquor out of it. We don't even permit it at all. And it's the most clean entertainment for the whole family.

Nora: *And the cheapest, exceptin' the clothes. Everyone of our costumes show full dresses, and we all wear slips and we all wear ruffled pantaloons.*

Interviewer: What's the general age range of most of the people that you clog with?

Nora: *About thirty-five to fifty-four.*

A number of the folks at the table tell you how much better they've felt physically ever since they took up clogging. What's more, it seems to be great for emotional well being:

Bob: *A lot of people who are very despondent over tragic events in their lives get into square dancing or clogging. People we talk into it will say they're glad we persisted. A police sergeant told me, "I have not felt so good and have not rested so well at night since I was a boy." And I know one fella who said, "Had it not been for this, my wife would have lost her mind."*

Interviewer: Do you enjoy square dancing and clogging equally?

Lendal: *We look forward to both of them but we enjoy clogging better. We enjoy promoting it more than you would think.*

Nora: *Well, you get applause when you clog, and when you square dance, everybody's doing it.*

Bob: *Of course, we use a lot of square dance routines in our clogging.*

Nora: *"Pass through," "star through," "right" and "left through."*

Lendal: *Oh yes. We have the same terminology in square dancing that we do in clogging.*

Interviewer: What do you call a group of eight couples?

Nora: *You call them "squares."*

Lendal: *In clogging you call them "teams."*

Bob: *And in square dancing you have a caller, while the round dance man is called a "cuer."*

Interviewer: What about cuing in clog dancing?

Nora: *It's supposed to be subtle, you know; we're supposed to hear 'em, but the audience is not supposed to know.*

Bob: *In clogging, your down beat is the heel beat. On a lot of*

other dances, your toe will tap out the rhythm; but in clogging, your heel is the heavy beat. Your upbeat will be a tap or toe.
Interviewer: How many basic steps are there?
Nora: *Actually, in clogging there's only eight basic steps. When you learn the eight basic steps, that's all of them. Then you can mix it together and come out with a bunch more. There's* toe, heel, step, drag, rock, slide, brush, *and* double toe.
Bob: *Those basics can work sideways, backwards, and forwards.*
Interviewer: Do you put round dancing in a different category?
Bob: *Well, yes. In a way it blends in with your square dancing field, because between each square dance tip you have what we call a "hash call," then a singing call, then the round dance call.*
Interviewer: Then you're talking about couples, not circles?
Bob: *I'm talking about couples. It's very much like ballroom dancing.*
Interviewer: So you two met over dancing (to Nora and Lendal).
Lendal: *Yes.*
Linda Fay [daughter]: *At least they have a mutual interest. When I go out with people, they don't want to go clogging. I say, "Well, you disco, and it's the same thing."*
Nora: *You should have seen us during the Veterans' Day Parade. I don't know how many thousands of people were there. And we had a float in the parade. They just ridiculed us. They laughed and giggled and hollered at us.*
Lendal: *We've had people and—their mouths fly open like that [demonstrating]—just stare at you. Well, it hurts us.*
Interviewer: Some folks need to be educated . . . .
Lendal: *That's what we're trying to do as promoters, I guess you might say.*
When we're on the floor, we're hollerin' and cuttin' up and carryin' on with each other; and sometimes it makes the audience feel like we're weird.
The pain of being misunderstood by outsiders seems more than compensated by the pleasure of folk group fellowship shared by the Town and Country dancers.
When the people don't start applauding us pretty soon, we

get in bad shape. You can see us and tell the difference.

Nora: *One Jubilee, when we first came out right on the edge, where we wouldn't be seen, you know, but the minute we joined hands and walked out, about three feet, everybody started clappin'. And they couldn't even see us good. And I said, "My God, they're clappin' and we're not even out there yet!" And I went into a trance, and I didn't remember nothin' through that whole routine. There were people clapping the whole time, and I don't think they ever quit.*

Actually we're together more than we are with our families. I haven't seen my mother in four weeks. We fuss just like we're all married to each other sometimes. And then it turns out we all agree on somethin'.

Lendal: *You meet one another; you compete with one another, you know. You don't do it to outshow, but for really fun, just for really fun.*

Bob: *But it does make you feel good when somebody walks up to you and says you're the best.*

Nora: *You know, that guy from the Logan Community Center, who said, "Ya'll got some of the 'goodest' steps I ever seen"? Best compliment we ever had. I said I wish he'd go tell the judges that. They didn't even know we was up there.*

Bob: *I think one of the things that people have missed more than anything else is personal fellowship. We used to sit around on the front porch in a rocking chair and the swings, and tell tall tales and all of the lore of yesterday. And I think we're getting back to this in many ways. You meet people all over the country; and if you've got this one thing in common, no matter what state they're from, if they're cloggers, you feel like you've known them all your life. You don't meet strangers.*

Nora: *That's the thing about it. You can go to any state you want to and if there is a club there, you're welcome to go and dance.*

Bob: *Like when we went to North Carolina. There'll be people there from Arkansas, Ohio—you'll feel like you've been knowing them for years.*

Lendal: *It's a national thing. It covers the world, too.*

The fiddlers strike up "Ragtime Annie," really putting the wood to it. Nora slides out of the booth at Louise's. Without her taps on, she does a little exhibition dance in the aisle. A receptive audience claps time and the eyes of the children outshine the fluorescents. Clogging hasn't just come to this area; it has *arrived!*

Discovering Folk Life-Styles

As a collector gaining in experience, you readily perceive aspects of folklore all around you—here, there, and everywhere; you realize that the bearers of folk traditions from whom you collect are quite often multi-faceted or multi-talented. You also understand the relationship of folkloric pursuits to regional, social, and biographical heritage. But only rarely do you expect to come upon folklore in a context in which folk tradition virtually prevails. The next harvesting excursions should give your collector's consciousness the necessary boost toward recognizing such golden opportunities to discover patterns of folk life-styles.

"Ma'cille's Museum of Miscellanea" is the intriguing message on an inconspicuous sign on the side of a Pickens County highway far from the nearest interstate. Its arrow leads you down a dirt road, along which you discover a place and a Southern way of life and some folks that add up to a folklore collector's heaven. You work your camera like never before and tape record for hours on end. You feel as though you need hardly seek further for the next few years, there's so much regional grassroots harvesting to captivate your attention—from traditional log buildings, rural artifacts, domestic life, to handicrafts, foodways, songs, tales, and dialect. And you hate to think of the friendships which might have gone uncultivated had collecting folklore not led you to Ma'cille and Daddy Norman House and their crowd of a family.

John Earl

In the House family there are four generations of self-sufficient folks who don't know the meaning of the word boredom. Conventionally involved in mainstream American community pursuits (from church attendance to PTA), the members of this family are also inextricably tied to region and their waste-not-want-not, do-it-yourself Southern agrarian folk heritage.

Ma'cille and Daddy Norman

Ma'cille and Daddy Norman House are, in fact, collectors nonpareil. As Ma'cille puts it—and for so doing should be up for an understatement-of-the-year award—*I was never one to throw anything away,* which goes for people as well as folk artifacts.

No one stays hungry or homeless who's fortunate enough to be around these folks. Ma'cille and Daddy Norman have six grown children, but there's no telling how many adoptions of the heart have occurred during their fifty-plus years of married life. Great grandparents several times over by now, they received their nicknames by means of that irrefutable logic to which only children seem to be privy. The "gran'kids" started calling Lucille House "Ma'cille," and their grandfather by the obviously complementary name of "Daddy Norman."

There's an actual homegrown museum of folklife and natural history on the House place, which Ma'cille and Daddy Norman make available to the public seven days a week and free of charge.

Since 1959, Ma'cille has pursued her avocation with enthusiasm, filling up buildings as fast as Daddy Norman, "retired" from construction work, can build them for her. Motivated by a desire to give her children opportunities the family otherwise could not afford, she taught them skills—lessons, in effect, in cultural anthropology, history, the arts—and generally, more about personal resourcefulness than they could have acquired under the most affluent of circumstances.

With her own never-idle hands, Ma'cille augmented a growing collection of rural artifacts by digging in the ground for antique dolls and bottles of every description. She taught herself taxidermy to produce a collection of wildlife and domestic animals that would do

Noah proud, and, among other things, she sews authentic replications of gowns worn by First Ladies for her treasured collection of dolls representing wives of all the Presidents of the United States.

As soon as you arrive at the Museum—really a compound of various buildings—you feel free to look around. Nothing is locked.

The museum is a bottle collector's paradise, rooms lined with every conceivable flask, jar, or jug—some novelties, many quite rare and beautiful.

It's not that Alabama contains only the virtuous, but folks think far too much of Ma'cille and Daddy Norman's hospitality and what they're trying to do for everybody to be taking anything away that doesn't belong to them.

Ma'cille will answer your question about security by remembering the *one time a lady did help herself to a little somethin' or other—a bottle, I believe it was. Well, we had quite a crowd that weekend, and I didn't even know it was gone before I found a package in the mail with a note apologizing to me. It was the bottle, and the lady who took it said she didn't know this museum is privately owned. She thought the state owned it!*

Where do all the dolls in Ma'cille's Doll House come from? Most of them Ma'cille and her family have found accidentally right in the ground.

Ma'cille points to the "Roanoke doll":

A lady made these dolls at the turn of the century. And, ah, she never gave her secret away—how she preserved its head. They're stockinette dolls, regular cloth dolls, but the head is as hard as papier-mâché. But she never gave her secret away— what she preserved it with.

You inquire about an interesting display shelf of small white porcelain dolls:

Back in the olden days, they were going for carriage rides, and the ladies wanted to look real nice. And they didn't want to put on coats and cover up their pretty dresses. One lady got so cold, she froze to death. And they called them "frozen Charlottes." But also, they're made together—I mean, they're not jointed; they're all in one piece. And, when they'd serve their tea at the ladies' tea parties, they would hand out these little dolls. And they stirred their tea [with them] and carried their little doll home as a souvenir.

Leaving the Doll House, you walk the country road past Ma'cille and Daddy Norman's residence, toward the main museum building. On a hot day you'll be invited in for iced tea; on a cold one, to warm yourself at their fire.

Nearing the Miscellanea Museum—the first building that Daddy Norman constructed for Ma'cille himself—you notice that the roof at your end is covered with bottles. Once clear, these bottles made at the turn of the century will turn violet from exposure to the sun.

The miscellanea collection inside the museum is fantastic for the care which Ma'cille obviously devotes to it. Anywhere you turn there are marvels to inspect.

There must be hundreds of examples in the museum, of animals great and small, on which Ma'cille has performed her own taxidermy.

The next building you come to is a dogtrot log house meticulously restored by Daddy Norman—an excellent carpenter with a conscientious regard for traditional practices in architecture. The

Marshal Hagler

Nearing the Miscellanea Museum—the first building that Daddy Norman constructed for Ma'cille himself—you notice that the roof at your end is covered
with bottles. Once clear, these bottles made at the turn of the century will
turn violet from exposure to the sun.

restoration is a synthesis of two relocated homes: flooring and
ceiling from one and logs from the Old Lancaster home, donated by
Verdo Elmore.

Indeed, Ma'cille has totally furnished the dogtrot home with
items from early settlement days in Alabama. Most everything has
been handed down to Ma'cille and Daddy Norman from their own
families less than five miles away from this site. One could move in.
The beds are made, rooms and cupboards are outfitted, spinning
wheel and loom are ready for use, ash hopper is filled out back,
even enough food is being raised nearby to supply an army, and the
Speed's Mill General Store is less than a minute's walk down the
road.

Daddy Norman explains: *The Speed's Mill Store came from
about seven miles down the road. There was an old water mill
down there. This is the third old store that was there at that*

Marshal Hagler

"The Speed's Mill Store came from about seven miles down the road. There was an old water mill down there. This is the third old store that was there at that particular place—Speed's Mill. It was about '30 or '31 when they built this store."

particular place—Speed's Mill. It was about '30 or '31 when they built this store.

It, too, is completely furnished and stocked, from its potbellied, woodburning stove and old Fairbanks scale to Octagon Soap (in the original packaging) and Grandma's Washing Powder (pronounced "warshing" around here) to buttons and spools of thread in those mahogany cases with the sliding glass doors (nowadays replaced by aluminum trees hung with merchandise in plastic bubbles).

Daddy Norman recalls the days of "white meat and kerosene":

Folks lived seven, eight to ten miles from town. And they'd go to that little ol' country store about twice a week, and buy 'em a dollar's worth of groceries: there'd be a pretty good wagonload for a dollar. If you didn't have a dollar to spend, you could carry a chicken and swap it for groceries.

The intense experience of your first tour is relieved not only by the beautiful country setting (the woods, flowers in bloom, birds, split rail fences, good-natured lethargic hounds, and noisy guineas) but also by countless touches of visual or verbal humor.

For the busloads of school children who come through on field trips, there's a tantalizing box in the main building marked "Baby Rattlers." Youngsters break up with laughter, upon cautiously lifting the lid, to find "rattlers" that babies play with.

And an equally tempting latched door to an exterior wall-mounted case warns ominously "Beware of White Bats." The child with initiative and mischief enough to sneak a look gets to make all the others laugh at the white baseball bats stored therein.

Daddy Norman points out the old tractor bought in 1927 and buggy purchased in 1906 that *cost me twenty-six dollars. That's what we paid at the time.*

Marshal Hagler

It, too, is completely furnished and stocked, from its pot-bellied, woodburning stove and old Fairbanks scale to Octagon Soap (in the original packaging) and Grandma's Washing Powder (pronounced "warshing" around here) to buttons and spools of thread in those mahogany cases with the sliding glass doors (nowadays replaced by aluminum trees hung with merchandise in plastic bubbles).

He shows you some cabbages and rutabagas of such ample dimensions that one alone would do a large family at mealtime.

His main crop? A toss up between turnip greens and Arsh potatoes: *Over five hundred bushel came out of that little ol' garden this summer.* No matter how hard the times, as he points out, there've always been enough strawberries or collards, English peas or Irish potatoes for the table, and often a few left over for the farmer's market.

He makes sorghum syrup on his place nearly every fall, you learn, and still uses mules to plow: Frank, Kate, and Dan. Patient, obedient old Dan will turn out to be your favorite months from now, but there's a lot to be said for Frank, too, as you find out momentarily, when you also get confirmation of your suspicion that Daddy Norman is an inveterate poker-faced yarn spinner:

Old Frank, I got him across the river, over in Greene County. I was over there one day, and a man was on him, and he was pointin' those birds. After Frank flushed the birds, the man'd shoot 'em, three or four of 'em. He'd go to pick 'em up. So I said, "I'm gonna buy that mule." He said, "OK, take three hundred dollars fer 'im." I said, "Well, I want the mule."

And so I started home and got down to the river, and he just balked. Wouldn't go no further. And the man, seein' what had happened, he came down there and said, "Hey, I forgot to tell you, the mule'd rather fish than to hunt!" And so I just happened to have one of them $19.95 Pocket Fishermen, and got right out there and caught five or six nice fish. Them bass weighed three or four pounds. I just hung 'em up on the mule and got on 'im, and he just waded across the river and came on home.

That's where the cabbage and the turnips come from. Ma'cille put Frank to the plow. And he was just a-fussin' and a-rearin'. And Ma'cille said, "He may know how to hunt, and he may like to fish, but he shore don't know nothin' about plowin'." And she tied the gate up. And down went the lines. "Whoah, haw, gee, Frank," she said. "It's all got to be plowed." And just whichever way Frank went is the way Ma'cille plowed.

It was a little rough, but she really got it broke up. I'll have to take it over from now on.

One big, happy family that's a folk group: On a sunny April Sunday—one of many delightful folklore collecting days spent at the House place—Ma'cille is in her kitchen hard at work and twice as cheerful. Family members are on their way from surrounding communities but also as far away as Nashville. The occasion, special though it may be, is an oft-repeated one: Sunday family dinner.

Oldest son Glenn, an artist who teaches printing (the traditional, painstaking way of setting type for beautiful books), shows you a new exhibit in the Doll House—Kachina dolls which he has made.

Glenn: *The Pueblos believe that every living thing has a spirit, or "Kachina" [They say Kah'-tzi-na, while we anglicize the term to Ka-tcheé-na], and that these spirits live either in the clouds or the mountains or the springs a certain part of the year. But in January they are said to come down and dwell among the Indians in the villages.*

And during this time the male adults take on outfits and masks to impersonate these Kachinas. Before the ceremonies, the uncles and the fathers make Kachina dolls, and during the ceremony they give these to the children as sort of a visual aid in learning about their religion.

When they hold their ceremonies, they give thanks, and they give their prayers for rain, good crops, and lots of children to the Kachinas to take back to the gods.

I've used some white pine and some fir, and one cottonwood root. I've managed now to find some cottonwood roots out here. The original Kachina dolls were made much more simply than any of these [pointing to his fully dimensional dolls, brightly painted and adorned with small feathers and, in some instances, bits of dried plantlife].

Interviewer: How did you get started making these?

Glenn: *I've been doing it for several years now. One Christmas Eve, I think in '72, my son and I decided to make a gift at the very* *last minute for my wife Virginia, and we found a pattern for one particular doll in a Boy Scout merit badge root carving book.*

Since then, Glenn has not only become well versed in Kachina lore, but has had an experience to add to it, which he lets you record for your collection:

That's "Alitáka," the cloud Kachina—this one over here [pointing]. This one isn't finished yet, and the reason for that is that the first one I made—when I put the last feather in the "tibletteh," it started raining, and rained for twenty-four hours without a letup. I didn't think too much about that.

About a year later, I made an identical doll. It started raining, rained for four days. The river "low" was thirty feet. I sent that doll to my friend in Texas. He was so taken by it that he called me immediately and thanked me. And I said, "How's the weather out there?" And he said, "It's raining. Why?" So I'm planning to wait until we have a long dry spell before I finish this one.

Just about everybody who's expected has arrived. Nobody steps out of car or truck without covered platters, trays, or armfuls of traditional Southern food. Ma'cille's been working since dawn, preparing casseroles (one featuring grits), homemade sausage, biscuits, vegetables, and a cake. To all this, add what comes in with each visiting family: platters of venison, fried chicken, cornbread, more vegetables in season and casseroles, gigantic slices of red ripe homegrown tomatoes, pickles, and six additional varieties of dessert. Come noon, everyone is told to "fill your plate and sit down to eat."

After dinner the children easily find their own amusements. There are trees to climb, baby chicks to visit, even a harmless snake to be relocated out of the way of traffic. Following a tradition that's been going on since the boys were small, as Ma'cille tells you, the men—sons, grandsons, in-laws—play dominoes out on the carport patio. The chores completed quickly by so many hands, the women gravitate to the front patio one by one. Dominoes click away; jokes are exchanged.

Daddy Norman, who is not playing this time, sits nearby, holding and stroking a frizzly chicken. Of course, several adoring children gather round. *This is a frizzly chicken* [He draws out the first vowel in *frizzly*]. *Now y'all know what a frizzly chicken looks like. His momma was a frizzly, his daddy was a frizzly, so he's a frizzly too. You know how you gotta eat a frizzly chicken, don't you? Left handed. You gotta eat a frizzly chicken left handed.*

Ma'cille joins Daddy Norman on the crowded porch. They sit together in the swing. Daddy Norman tells how he courted Ma'cille more than fifty years ago on the advice of his best friend whose own wife had run out on him: *He told me to get myself an ugly wife "so she'll stay home, and won't leave you," and that's just what I did. I got me an ugly wife.* Ma'cille doesn't seem to mind the teasing, sees right through it, as a matter of fact. She knows how Daddy Norman really feels about his childhood sweetheart.

Daddy Norman has had old Dan all hitched up to the wagon since before dinner. Now he's fixing to give more than a dozen kids a ride around the place. From the driver's seat, while he waits for them all to pile in, he tells you the story about the "cherries":

I was raised by a stepfather, but my grandfather was still livin'. Coming back from a trip to Louisiana with my Gran'paw, he'd got his eatin' money down to fifty cents. And he seen where you could get all you could eat for twenty-five cents. And he said, "We'll eat up enough to do us till we get back to Gordo."

We went in there and the lady said, "Well, the food's not hardly done yet. But sit down, and I'll give you some coffee and tea." And they had a big pot, a big dish, there, with little pickled peppers in it. I thought it was cherries. I put it in my mouth, and tears started comin' out of my eyes.

And Gran'paw said, "Why art thou crying, son?" I said, "Gran'paw, just ignore me." I said, "Have a cherry, Grandfather." Gran'paw got three of them cherries and put them in his mouth and stood there hollerin'. That pepper was burnin' him down to his gizzard. And then I said, "Gran'paw, how come thou art crying?" He said, "Cause, you little rascal, you didn't die forty-one years ago when your daddy did!"

While Daddy Norman takes his wagonload of kids for a ride out to the garden, the game comes to an end and gives way to informal

John Earl

Ma'cille joins Daddy Norman on the crowded porch.

conversation. Youngest son Jerry unpacks his guitar, tunes up, and settles in the swing to play quietly. Encouraged by his wife Faye, Jerry now lives in Nashville, so he can be near the music industry when they discover what is common knowledge around here—that Jerry sings better than most and writes the best tunes ever, filling his songs with humor, tradition, and human warmth:

A lot of people ask me, "What's your favorite song you've written?" And I always have to tell 'em it's, ah, "Reverend-Everett-Beverly-and-Sister-Anna-Laura [pronounced like Anna

Laur']-Sung-a-Fa-Sol-La-Song-Down-at-Salem-Church-Last-Sunday-from-Twelve-O'Clock-to-Six-O'Clock-that-Night-and-Little-Sister-Turned-Blue-in-the-Face-from-Singin'-Too-High-and-They-Had-to-Tote-Her-Down-to-the-Spring-and-Splash-Cold-Water-on-Her-To-Make-Her-Wake-Up" [chuckle]! *It's the only song I ever wrote from a dream. And that's why I like it so much, I reckon, because I know I didn't have to work so hard for it.*

It was way down deep South durin'
Reconstruction days,
When everybody needed help in
Every kind of way.
Travellin' in an oxen cart,
A-pickin' an old guitar,
Came the Reverend Everett Beverly
And his sister Anna Laura.

They went to all-day singin's
With the dinners on the ground.
When Sister Anna Laur' would sing,
No one could quieten her down.
Well, the folks would spread the word around and
They'd come from near and far,
To hear the Reverend Everett Beverly
And his sister Anna Laura.

Fa mi sol sol la,
Fa mi sol sol la,
Fa sol sol la fa sol.
Sing the fa so high,
And the sol so low.
Fa mi sol sol la fa sol!

When they would lead the singin',
Folks follered them out of town.
They kept on a-wantin' to hear them sing

Them good soul savin' sounds,
'Cause their songs echoed the valleys
Just like a heavenly choir,
The Reverend Everett Beverly
And his sister Anna Laura.

For years and years they travelled,
And their singing was heard.
While Sister Anna Laura did sing,
The Reverend spread the word.
And family recollections
Remember who they are.
It's great, great grandpa Beverly,
And his sister Anna Laura!

Fa mi sol sol la,
Fa mi sol sol la,
Fa sol sol la fa sol.
Sing the fa so high,
And the sol so low—
                          ow.
Fa mi sol sol la fa sol!

Dogs stretch out lazily on the grass. A toddler and her even younger baby sister join hands to dance a little jig while Jerry performs several more lively numbers with a lot of chin music, or "Diddling," in them.

Today Daddy Norman is wearing one white sneaker and one black dress shoe [the latter, that half of a grandson's gift which does not pinch]. Everytime he's asked about it, though, Daddy Norman patiently explains it's *so everyone will know that I got two pairs, one for Sunday and one for every day.* True to his heritage, oldest son Glenn responds, *I'll bet you have another pair up at the house just like 'em!*

A late afternoon stroll takes us to the dogtrot log house, where Daddy Norman sits down in the rocker by the fireplace. The old churn which Ma'cille has placed within reach evokes first a family anecdote (legend) and then a folktale.

My brother, he done the churnin'. You're supposed to do this-a-way.

Daddy Norman demonstrates the conventional up and down churning motions produced by the hand held dasher.

But he liked to read comic books, when comic books first come out—"Mutt 'n Jeff" and what have you. And now, Mother went to the garden and picked some peas or beans or turnip greens or some kind of vegetable, and left him with the churnin'. And when she got back, he about had the butter gathered, but he wasn't churning with his hands.

Daddy Norman leans down, and, before you know it, has removed a shoe and sock.

Well, he didn't have on any shoes. I don't like 'em. I wouldn't have had none today if it had not a-been Mothers' Day, and that boy hadn't brought me a pair of shoes today for Mothers' Day.

When my mother came back from the garden with her peas or beans or whatever squashes she had, this boy was sitting there with his foot on the thing.

Daddy Norman demonstrates. Placing the dasher between the big and second toes of his bare foot, he simulates the process—the churning leg neatly crossed over the idle one, which serves as a prop.

He was reading his comic books. When Mother got through with him with a board, he never did churn with his foot no more. He always had his hands there; he was sorry he put his toes up thar.

Still barefoot and rocking, Daddy Norman launches into his second story:

We didn't have no refrigerator; didn't even have no ice box. We kept our milk in a spring. Had a little house over the spring, and, ah, had a little old kerosene lamp on the table. It was quite dark in there, and it done got darker in there. And Mother poured me a big old goblet of buttermilk.

And I kept lookin' at it and lookin' at it, and she said, "Son," said "Honey, do you see somethin' in your milk?"

I said, "Yes Ma'm, Mother," and I said, "He sees me, too." And he started wallerin' around, swimmin' in that glass of milk. And he got him a little ball of butter, and he was sittin' up on there on that little ball of butter. I said, "Yes Ma'm, there's somethin' in my milk, and," I said, "he sees, me, too!"

And she taken him out of there just as easy, but she stripped all that milk off of him. And I said, "I drank that milk." And she said, "Boy, it ain't nasty." It was a little frog.

Well, she kept him around there for several years. When the milk had clabbered and she'd get rid of the dasher, she'd call, "Come here, Oscar!" And he'd come a-leapin' and a-leapin', and she'd take the cloths off the churn and the lid off, and he'd whoof into that churn. And she let him swim around in there, where he got the butter made and the milk churned.

He'd get up on a little butter—he had some kind of way of talkin' to her, that frog talk. She could understand it. She'd go and help him out. She'd say, "Come here, Oscar. Now you didn't take nothin' in there and you ain't gonna bring nothin' out," and she'd strip all that milk off him before she took him out.

She'd turn him a-loose, and he'd play around and eat bugs and anything that he could find, until the next day. Gettin' ready to churn, she'd say, "Come here, Oscar!" And he'd come a-leapin'. He thought he was going to get to take a bath in . . . mother's milk; looks like the frog enjoyed it.

And finally, he got so old till he got arther-itis in the joints of his legs, and he just wasn't able to do it no more. And she carried him to the river and turned him a-loose. She said, "You can just go free now, 'cause you churned a million churns of butter and milk by now." And that was the end of the frog churnin' tale.

As many times as that little frog helped Daddy Norman's mother do the churning must be the number of times Ma'cille has baked her crowd-pleasing biscuits. On this well-fed Sunday, she has decided to *just fix a light supper of sausage and biscuits. I know there's nothin' they'd rather eat.* She's right, of course, and you collect the process:

You have some flour. Some means a good sized dough tray full. Ma'cille makes a well in the flour with the fist of her right hand and pours half a glass of buttermilk and half a glass of water into the cavity. She "works" the dough with the one hand, proceeding very gradually from the center to the periphery of the dough bowl. *Just work it a little bit at a time.* She stops to grease a baking pan with lard (using her left hand), adds about half a cup to the dough, then continues to work it: *I've made 'em all over this country, because everywhere I go, they make me make 'em. I get lots of practice at it. My grandmother learned me how to make biscuits when I was about nine years old. The boys once had a contest to see who could eat the most at one meal.* The winner ate seventeen.

The dough is about ready. *If I feel I can handle it good, you know, without it sticking all over my hands, it's right.* She pinches off the dough and forms each biscuit by hand, arranging them on a pie plate and baking sheets. As she pops them into her kitchen oven (at five hundred degrees—she believes in cooking them quickly), she observes that folks like the romance of eating biscuits baked in a woodburning stove. Ma'cille has made hundreds that way, especially at arts and crafts festivals. But she believes they taste just as good baked "in a regular oven."

No one has moved farther than fifteen feet from the stove all this time. The quiet spoken words which summon all to come and eat serve equally to sum up the day: *It's right.*

Choctaw Natural Garden: One Thousand Years at the Same Location

The Houses generously open their museum to the community-at-large. Grassroots self-sufficiency and self-reliance seem to make for a great deal of selflessness. In Pearl River, where kinship and community are one, the elderly, for example, are never set aside as burdensome or inconsequential. An ethnic subculture, in many respects set apart from mainstream America, the Choctaw community is a folklife group—a folk group as organically integrated as the traditional garden we are going to visit.

With the exception of facilities like crafts gift shops (and much like the House premises), Indian reservations are not public turf. So unless the public has been invited to a reservation festival (in which case one proceeds in the manner of any guest at someone else's home), it's a good idea to phone the tribal office to let folks know you'd appreciate permission to visit. Courtesy insures not only your welcome but help in locating people to talk with and places to see.

You might even find yourself invited to stay late, have hominy and chicken for supper, and come to the powwow planned for that night. That's precisely the kind of hospitality you'll encounter at the Pearl River community of Choctaw Indians near Philadelphia, Mississippi.

That there are Indians in Mississippi was finally recognized by Congress in 1918, as you'll learn from Bob Ferguson, an "Anglo" who demonstrates that there are white men who choose to live at Pearl River. *The Choctaws were just a scattered remnant, and they resisted the 1880s removal, even the last effort in 1900.* It's amazing how much you can learn during a brief visit—providing you don't confuse your role with that of an anthropologist in residence. There are questions it is not one's place to ask, that even an anthropologist in residence would not wish to answer, as Bob Ferguson implies:

My ties are strong with this tribe. The reason I went back to college and did my graduate work in anthropology is that I was learning things that were wrong in the books, and I wanted to write legitimately for the ethnographers to read. I've published some. And then after I got to knowing the people better and their culture, I didn't want to write certain things. They were in sacred trust. And so I turned down the Smithsonian and all that.

Sometime, after the people are all dead, OK, but not now, you know?

Bob is happy to explain how the Mississippi Choctaw remarkably has maintained cultural continuity with the past.

Back in DeSoto's time the Choctaws were a very powerful tribe. They had a trade route all the way from the Mobile area, up through the Natchez Trace, on up into Iroquois country. The language spoken was called Mobilian. The Indians in the Southeast were an orderly civilization, you know. There were natural boundaries. There were buffer zones between these boundaries. There were hunting areas that were designated as such by many tribes. For example, the Kentucky-Tennessee area was a hunting ground respected by eighteen tribes. Nobody lived there.

And one of the great tribes of the South was the Choctaws. And they were the prime agricultural Indians. Other tribes like the Chickasaw, which speak the same language, traded hides, fresh meat, and that sort of thing to the Choctaws for garden produce. Corn, beans, squash, and so on. Many of the Choctaws here now became sharecroppers or the sons of sharecroppers when they had to go underground because they lost their land and decided to stay here.

In 1830, the tribe went West, the government went West, the missionaries went West. But an intensive Choctaw culture survives in Mississippi. Those who chose to stay retained the old culture, while the Oklahoma Indians assimilated.

Bob Ferguson is from Missouri; he met his wife, a Choctaw, in Chattanooga, Tennessee, and they lived in Nashville until last year. What brings him to Pearl River? He's teaching organic gardening here:

I was raised on a farm, and then a few years ago I threw away my chemicals. In Nashville, I was in the music business. I was a song writer, and I was in conservation. I had a hit or two that got me into music heavy. I produced Chet Atkins and fifty other artists while I was there. But this was just a lot more important. A lot of people are lining up to make records and not so many are lining up to teach gardening.

Why do the Choctaws with their great agricultural heritage need to be taught anything about gardening? Because in one important respect, the continuity with their agricultural past was broken.

The tragedy in the Southeastern tribes was not the removal itself, but what it stood for. From 1800 to 1830, they had made a conscious effort to become acceptable to the American people. They had fought for the United States, they had fought the Battle of New Orleans, they had fought against the Creeks, against Tecumseh. They adopted as they could all American standards of the times. They started schools; they passed laws getting rid of the blood revenge. And then still they were rejected as not being eligible to become American citizens.

This is the tragedy. As Pushmataha, one of the great leaders said, "This tribe has held the hands of the United States so long that her nails are grown long like the talons of a bird, and we could not let go if we wanted to." They had consciously chosen to be partners with the U.S. So they took up plow agriculture, and that broke the continuity with the old Indian agriculture.

Bob is doing his part in repaying a debt, by showing his adopted people just how right was their traditional use of land. The small, experimental garden he shows you has you so convinced of the beauty and simplicity and effectiveness of traditional gardening that you find it hard to believe how seldom it is practiced.

The first thing you notice is a marigold bed in a vegetable garden. Says Bob, *The marigolds are there to keep away the nematodes.* How so?

Marigolds put out a substance in the soil which is toxic to nematodes, keeping them away from the root area in a two-foot circle for two years. Even when they're finished, we put 'em down into the ground, flower and all. You can plant several different flowers. Nasturtium is an attraction plant. It will pull aphids away from other plants.

You can grow a lot of flowers in your vegetable garden. Daisies are deadly to insects. You can really have a pretty garden at the same time that you grow your food.

That seems doubly true about the sunflowers or, if you prefer,

"Jerusalem artichokes," which are edible as well as pretty. The latter name comes from the Italian word *girasole* (meaning "sunflower"). You and Bob talk about this interesting bit of folk etymology—that folk custom of misconstruing a meaningless sound like *girasole* or *asparagus* into a meaningful one like "Jerusalem artichoke" or "sparrow grass" (thus contributing to an informal vocabulary that circulates right alongside, or even replaces, its formal counterpart). Bob knows a good bit of sunflower lore: *I have not yet found out the Indian name for it, but the Jerusalem artichoke is an American Indian sunflower. It will grow big and tall and have flowers, but it has tuberous roots just like potatoes, and these tubers are what you harvest and eat. And they're very good food. Raw, you can cut 'em up in salad. You can fry 'em like potatoes, boil 'em.*

Diabetics can eat 'em without any concern. And they sell for a dollar to a dollar and a half for a small package at the stores nowadays. They're on the market now as "sunchokes." You go into a little store and you find sunchokes.

Marigolds and sunchokes are interesting enough, but there are two miracles in Bob Ferguson's demonstration garden. The first is the compost ring, constructed of wire fencing.

Bob Ferguson explains: *Our compost ring is the heart of the organic system. You just leave it up, and plant tomatoes around it. When it rains, the compost in the ring collects moisture. The nutrients wash down through there and feed your tomatoes.*

And that brings you around to the second miracle in Bob's thousand-year-old garden: hay mulch grown potatoes. You walk over to the rows, and Bob points to three sections, each of which has been planted a different way, so that his fifteen Choctaw students, who meet here every Saturday, can *draw their own conclusions, you know.* The students and he *scraped up topsoil to make the hill for the potato beds.*

We turned it and used a colloidal phosphate from Florida. The basic nutrients are nitrogen, phosphorous and potash. This is a long term, slow release, natural material, and these applications, unlike chemicals, last five to ten years each. Once you

John Earl

"Our compost ring is the heart of the organic system. You just leave it up, and the next spring, move your wire to a new location. And just spread that out right there. This is one way that you build the organic content of your soil."

get your hay mulch built up heavy, you can use less and less of that. You can even arrive at the point where you don't have to add anything but hay.

The most interesting row has no dirt cover at all: *The potato is planted on top of the dirt, and then it's covered with hay and mulched some more and mulched some more. You'll be able to reach in pretty soon and pick the potatoes right in the hay; you don't have to dig 'em.*

My garden in Nashville got to the point where all I had to do was part my hay each spring, and make my rows with my finger and just plant 'em. Organic gardening is the oldest form of gardening in the world. Yet a scientific study of it is still new.

Ten home gardens have been started already, and everything grown in the demonstration garden goes on the menus for the nutrition program for the elderly. Eventually, it is Bob Ferguson's dream to see every Choctaw household that wishes it to have a self-sufficient mulch-ring garden beside the house, with plenty for the table and surplus for a farmer's market.

The idea of this program is that it's a reservation-based program. It can lead to an important economy for the tribe. If you have a good, sound basis, then you can foresee salesman's jobs, managerial, secretarial, trucking, everything—but all based on the land and not predicated on removal to Cincinatti, or San Francisco or something like that. It starts in your own backyard.

You comment on the number of churches you passed on your way over to see Bob, and he tells you, _Lots of 'em are church members and a lot of 'em are Baptists. He grins: One old Indian was baptized. And he came back later to be de-baptized 'cause he couldn't kill any more deer. So he got de-baptized and was able to hunt deer again!_

Then, more seriously, he explains, _There are cases where the Choctaws will have a synchronous event, like they will have a Choctaw ceremony and then go into the church and have the Christian wedding ceremony._

You remember to ask about this later when you talk to Choctaw artist Robert Billie, whose wedding took place three weeks ago:

In the Anglo tradition, it's always the bride's family that prepares the wedding feast, but in the Indian tradition everybody brings the food. A Choctaw wedding is when all the relatives bring food and gifts. They have the opening of the gifts and they sit down to eat afterwards. It's bad luck to have it in the house; you have to have it in a different place. Here, we use the Community Hall.

The Choctaw wedding required witnesses as in Anglo tradition. In the old days it used to be the entire village. In the old days, the man took on the woman's family name. No more today, because it would be going against Mississippi law. A man and a woman couldn't marry within their clan. That went against Choctaw law.

The Choctaw ceremony consists of getting the "OK" from the chiefs. The man used to have to talk to the chief of his own clan, and his chief would talk to the chief of the other clan. That *chief would talk to the woman's mother. Now they symbolize that in a handshake—a handholding ceremony. Now they pledge each other. My wife did it her way, and I did it my way. All of it took place in church.*

At the arts and crafts building, with its gift shop, from Linda Farve, who's in charge, you learn about the rabbit sticks traditionally used to club rabbits, when at least twelve people would hunt together, sheer numbers and skill making it possible to surround the rabbits in order to club them, without the use of a net.

Hickory stickball rackets (Kapucha) and golf ball size stickballs—goat or deer hide strips wound tightly around a rubber core—are redolent of passionately fought games, sometimes lasting for days on end, even to serve as a substitute for war in settling disputes. Nowadays, the Choctaws feel about stickball much as "Anglos" about football or soccer; but games are held mostly on special occasions like the annual July "Green Corn Dance" celebration turned "Choctaw Indian Fair" and opened to the public.

In the past, Choctaw basketry was a craft—a utilitarian necessity. Today it is an art form, Linda Farve explains: *Among the Choctaws it is traditionally a woman's job. The women who do it have learned it from their mothers. It takes quite a bit of time to learn. The baskets are made of swamp cane, which looks like a fishing pole. The cane is obtained from any swampy area or the edge of a river. There are about three kinds of the bamboo or swamp cane. But the cane harvested near water is more flexible. With a sharp knife, they cut it down, and then bring it in. And they split the canes into half and then fourths, and then they cut the top off. They used to dye the baskets with blood roots or hickory bark or plum roots, but now they just use commercial dyes. To get the different shapes, they count the canes, and it comes up the different shapes and designs. They just bend the swamp cane into shape.*

Cane baskets come in all shapes and sizes. To see someone double weaving a cane basket to produce a finished basket inside and out, in one continuous weave, is to be forever impressed by the high degree of its maker's skill.

At the powwow, native dancing follows an informal community meal. Floodlights turn night into day, and this is one time when no folklore collector wants to be without a camera to photograph folks from all seven Mississippi Choctaw communities—from children to elders—doing snake dances; duck dances; medium war dances; lively, fast war dances; and "stealing partners." The tape recorder comes in handy too. To Anglo ears at first unable to discern the breadth of musical range in modes of Choctaw chants, the familiarity acquired through playback later on converts the strange to the beautiful and familiar.

Men and boys wear the traditional ribbon shirts they now only put on for special occasions. Mothers and daughters have on the complementary aproned dresses which most of the Choctaw matrons wear daily. Beaded collars and jeweled haircombs give the women and girls a festive air. Shirts, dresses, collars, combs—the native finery is exquisitely handfashioned.

It can take a month or more to sew a single dress, for the tiers and tiers of diamond appliqué or the rows of black crosses and circles (to represent sticks and stickballs) are formed from bits of ribbon, torn

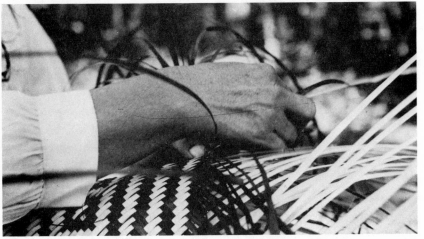

Courtesy of Choctaw Community News, Philadelphia, Mississippi

In the past, Choctaw basketry was a craft—a utilitarian necessity. Today it is an art form.

John Earl

Special occasions like the annual July "Green Corn Dance" celebration turned "Choctaw Indian Fair" are open to the public.

by hand and folded under, piece by piece, into the desired shapes before being sewn to the cloth.

The duck and snake dances are tributes, by imitation, to traditional natural allies—sources of food and habiliments.

"Stealing partners" brings on general mirth, no matter how many times it is danced throughout the evening, for the humor, rarely based on the same situation twice, depends on who steals himself which partner and how far away from his former place in the circle he must travel, for sometimes before a boy or man can return there with his new partner, she is "stolen" from him to peals of laughter from onlookers.

The fast war dance is the liveliest of the Choctaw dances, though there seems nothing hostile about it. Women participate, too, though their steps are more subdued than their male partners'.

Flamboyant costumes with bells, feathered bustles, and leggings remind you more of storybook images than the gentle folks with whom you've spent this memorable day.

John Earl

It wouldn't be a powwow without a hominy and chicken supper in the Community Center.

Folk Artists: A Study in Contrast

The local, usually annual, folk festival or arts and crafts fair which features the folk arts (even if not exclusively) is a good base from which to make contacts with talented resource people and even to begin impromptu interviewing.

As the excerpts of interviews which follow demonstrate, differences in degree of contact affect the kind and scope of the harvest. When you find yourself in the fortunate position of being able to maintain regular contact with someone like Jimmy Lee Sudduth, you will have an inexhaustible resource. But you can also make the most of even a single brief encounter with someone as vivacious as Lida Holley. And as introspective and articulate a source as Johnny Shines can bring you to a certain depth of perception in relatively few contact hours.

The active folklore collector becomes as sensitive to differences as to similarities. If you have noted similar qualities of human spirit inherent in the variety of folklife explored thus far, you will eventually discover prominent differences in the points of view and temperaments of folks involved in a relatively constant cultural scene.

If the artists of this world, who have always been considered an uncommon lot, do have one thing in common, it is likely to be the fact of their respective individuality. The general public is perennially fascinated by the uncommon personalities of elite and popular artists (whose biographies sometimes upstage the content of their works). The folklore collector will be unable to dismiss a similar fascination for the peculiarities of grassroots artists and performers—the variety of their objectives and complexity of emotions.

Jimmy Lee Sudduth, Folk Artist

There is every reason to linger at folk painter Jimmy Lee Sudduth's display at an annual festival close to home. But only later, on follow-up visits with Jimmy Lee, do you get to watch him paint, or hear him play his music, or become familiar with his life-style, or do you really get to know him and his wife as fully dimensional people, or become privy to Jimmy Lee's unique impressions of the national folk festival in which he participated by special invitation.

A black man, now in his early seventies, Jimmy Lee grew up in rural Fayette County but today lives right in the heart of the town also called Fayette. Like most of the folks you meet while collecting, Jimmy Lee Sudduth has mastered many skills, including the art of living.

He's an extraordinary folk painter, a self-taught artist, who has developed his God-given talent informally, improving his craft with every passing year in the "school" of nature and daily experience. A fine instrumental folk musician as well, Jimmy Lee plays the "French harp," perhaps more widely known as the harmonica.

Jimmy Lee makes all his own colors. When he was very young, his family was too poor to afford paints, so nature became the storehouse of his art supplies. He can paint a locomotive to look so real you expect to hear it whistle, which you will if he happens to be blowing his French harp while you're gazing at it. For he can make his harp sound like a locomotive and the rest of the train to boot.

He takes his subjects mostly from life, especially when they derive from his immediate environment. But he is not averse to inspiration from a magazine picture or from his own memory. His paintings as well as his music reflect a point of view as remote from censure or complaint as affirmation will allow. Jimmy Lee Sudduth is himself an original. He's a man who looks life straight in the eye and tells it an unequivocal *yes*. His capacity for joy derives

Jimmy Lee Sudduth

precisely from a spirit that has prevailed over hard times, sad times, and has triumphed.

When you first met Jimmy Lee (he was sixty-five then), it delighted you to hear him say, "I'm gonna be *fay-mous, fay-mous!*" and then laugh, as much at himself for saying it as with the joy of conviction that he deserved to be saying it. Since then, he may not have become famous in your sense of the word, but his reputation has grown to the point where he cannot keep his paintings around much longer than it takes for them to dry out.

Collectors like to ask Jimmy Lee to sign the paintings they buy from him. Jimmy Lee, who's had about as much formal schooling as most seventy-year-old black men who grew up in the deep South, is happy to oblige. He usually signs "Jimmy Lee Suddth," omitting the vowel in an act of phonetic logic never thwarted in any classroom.

Jimmy Lee enjoys going public. He is thrilled by attention from local reporters or an occasional TV interviewer. He welcomes visits to his home by art lovers. No one supports the arts more generously than Jimmy Lee himself. To see him wax enthusiastic about the work of another painter or craftsperson, who might well be competing with him for attention, sales, or even an achievement award, is enough to renew one's faith in spiritual brotherhood.

Look at that! Did you ever see anything so fine? Look at these colors; right over here, see? Boy, I'm tellin' you that's beautiful! And before you know it, he'll have swapped one of his own paintings (probably valued considerably higher in fine arts circles) for a sample of the admired artist's work to take home and cherish.

In an early conversation taped with Jimmy Lee, you say:

I hear you weren't but eight years old when you first started painting.

Jimmy Lee: *I was. One day I was lonesome, you know, and I started on the ground. I made a painting on the ground. Later I got some colorings, you know, and commenced paintin' on a board. And I got me some grass and some weeds and stuff, and you know, rubbed the color on—on a brick. So I thought I'd put it on my paintings, you know. And so I put it on my painting, and it looked good, and I just loved it. And so I've been painting practically half a hundred years!*

His "canvasses" are really wooden boards, metal sheets, tin lids, any and all "found objects" with flat surfaces hospitable to his particular variety of "paints," sometimes even concrete block walls.

Interviewer: Jimmy Lee, tell me some of the ingredients that you use to make your colors.

Jimmy Lee: *Coffee, sugar—when the old lady ain't around [laughing]—I use a little bit of everything. Flour—I get in the meal barrel, you know, while she's away—and I use a little*

Jimmy Lee's tapered fingers are his finest painting implements.

tobakker—tobacco leaves, you know—old homemade to-bacco. Press it all together and rub it and then it makes color. Eggs—I use the yellow of eggs. I use matches—take a match and strike it, you know, and it makes the color of smoke, like real smoke [in paintings depicting locomotives or chimneys], like the hair on that girl's head over there [referring to his nearby portrait of a woman].

Interviewer: Coca-Cola? Shoe polish?

Jimmy Lee: *I use so many things I can't hardly think of them myself.*

Interviewer: And greens, all different kinds of greens . . .

Jimmy Lee: *Turnip greens, that's right. Cabbage leaves. Everything that makes color.*

Together you take a close look at some of the paintings while Jimmy Lee explains their composition:

Jimmy Lee: *Now, this is grass. You just rub it up and down on the wood, just like that. See, it'll cut that into the grain of wood. This is mud right here, from the railroad, the Southern Railroad, you know, like smoke?*

One features a log house in careful detail:

Jimmy Lee: *Well, now, look here. This is my finger [placing it over a log and duplicating the stroking motions he used to form the logs]. See where that fits on the logs? I put the white first [referring to the chinking between the logs], and that white is flour, what's in biscuits. And I picked up this here mud, and just made a mark just like this [demonstrating how each log is made separately]. And you got to go over and over it again before you get it built up.*

Interviewer: May I touch?

Jimmy Lee: *Tetch.*

Interviewer: It feels very smooth [surprised at the evenness of the highly built-up surface and how firmly the homemade paintstuffs adhere to the wood].

Jimmy Lee: *This is eggs [pointing to touches of yellow amidst the greenery]. See how yellow that is there?*

Interviewer: Yes. There are numerous shadings of yellow greens, yellows, rust tones [saying aloud what you want the tape recorder to remind you about later].

Nowadays, he's best known for his paintings of log houses, dug wells, covered bridges, or other symbols of traditional Southern country life. But he paints human subjects, landscapes, or the geometric intricacies of large urban buildings with equal enthusiasm.

Jimmy Lee: *And then I take my pocket knife—I won't take it out 'cause the sheriff's likely to get me—and I scratch it, I scratch it like that, you know.*

You move to another painting. The subject, which fills a fifteen by thirty-inch plywood surface, is a weatherboarded one and one-half story, third generation "double pen" folk house. It has upper windows at the front, a closed-in displaced porch, and the traditional exterior chimney at each gable. The perspective is a forty-five degree angle from the front and center.

Jimmy Lee: *I took a fork to this [pointing to the striations on the roofs of house and porch]. And this is coffee [referring to the densely wooded background] and grass.*

Interviewer: I notice three different shades of clay for the boards, the roof, and the chimneys. Where did you find this pinker shade for the roof?

Jimmy Lee: *Well, I got that off my sister Anna Lou's place. She told me I could go down there and dig all I want. This [pointing to the chimneys and foundation] is red clay. You don't get that clay no more around here, I don't guess. It's red just like blood, you know, very red. And this [the clay used to "paint" the clapboarding] is the yellow that's at home—the yellow clay, you know. You got to be quick with it.*

He has a jar of mud handy and a small piece of board. He demonstrates, starting a log cabin while you watch. He uses a pencil to outline the logs, and some fresh picked greens:

Well, this is "poke salit." Good to eat! And this is where you get the mud out of the poke salit and put it on the building!

In the summer of '76, Jimmy Lee Sudduth was one of the five thousand and some musicians and craftspeople from the United States and thirty-six other nations who were invited to participate in the Smithsonian Institution's Festival of American Folklife—a "living museum" as it was called. The festival took place on the Washington, DC Mall, between the Lincoln Memorial and the Washington Monument, from June 16 through September 6.

Each participating artist was a guest in the city for two weeks. Jimmy Lee was privileged to be flown there over the fourth of July.

An imposing turn-of-the-century hotel Jimmy Lee noticed while traveling through a large city.

Hundreds of thousands of visitors attended the birthday celebration that summer, while as many more wished they could have come, too. Jimmy Lee's firsthand account is a fitting tribute to a momentous event by one *of* the people who was there *for* the people.

Interviewer: Jimmy Lee, you must have painted a lot of pictures while you were in Washington.

Jimmy Lee: *They wouldn't let me draw a picture till the two last days! Two last days. I had to hustle. I couldn't show 'em. They wanted me to entertain, and don't even show 'em till the last day.*

Interviewer: You mean, they had you playing music?

Jimmy Lee: *That's right. I was up on the stage. I was blowin' the*

French harp on the stage, and it seated eight hundred there when I played the second day, and they were playing that song, "Now I'll Fly Away," and I was blowin' on my harp.

Boy, they put me on camera up there. It was somethin'; I'll tell you. And then I didn't get to go across half of it—I seen a fifth of the exhibits up there. I had some fun. I didn't carry but two harps, though.

Blessed with the ability to unwrap each new day like a child with a birthday gift, gleefully anticipating the surprise bound to be contained therein, Jimmy Lee is not often disappointed.

Jimmy Lee: *Boy, it was wonderful. I'm tellin' you, ooh, they served me some of the best food! I just loved it.*

At the White House—close to the White House—they had a tent, you know, a long tent that could feed eight hundred at one meal. But there was seventy-five thousand up there the last day. Seventy-five thousand!

Boy, there wasn't nothin' but heads. That's the fourth of July. There wasn't nothin' but heads. Boy, oh, now some of them shoot them candles on the river, you know, what d'you call 'em?

Interviewer: Sky rockets, fireworks?

Jimmy Lee: *Oooh goodness! Prettiest things you ever seen. Some of 'em burst and they'd fly off. Next day I walked back up over there and looked at them trees over there, 'cause I believe that scorched them trees. That smoke's gonna kill them trees.*

You reassure him that the cherry trees in Washington are at this moment in full bloom.

Jimmy Lee: *I'd love to have seen that. I'd have loved to walk down to Washington. I didn't even get to go no further than the Capitol; I could see way down that avenue, but here'd come a bunch of different people. And these other kind of people that talks this funny talk and has these bells around their legs. [Here Jimmy Lee imitates the sound of a foreign language.] I just had to point at my pictures, you know. They got in with us. I don't know what you call them.*

And then that last day, oooh ooh! I was just shocked over how it come out like it did.

Interviewer: So, what happened the last day? How did you show the pictures?

Jimmy Lee: *They give me the last day. And I had to quit! I run out of pictures then. That's the truth. I didn't have enough. They were buyin' them things like nobody's business.*

And they had a sorghum mill, you know, where they mix syrup, going around and round. And I went up there and got that syrup, you know? And the man who give me the syrup said, "Oh, you can't make nothin' out of that!" I said, "Sure. I'm gonna paint a picture." He said, "I got to see that."

I stirred it up in the mud, you know, and got it started. And I painted a picture on the President's barn. Great big thing. I had to do it quick, you know. I drawed it this big [gesturing expansively]. But I had to dip this dirt with my hand. A fella I talked to the other day saw it and it's still up on the wall. Said it looked like I just painted it. Rained on it.

Interviewer: Now, where did you say you painted it?

Jimmy Lee: *There in the art place, that barn, there, where we were. You know, there was one white barn, and another red barn on the other side is the barn where they have the library, you know. I was over there at that place.*

And so the police put us over there. They had to put a string around me. I couldn't even draw no pictures, you know. Those folks, they'd get around, and he said they ought to put a string around to keep them back.

I said, "Well, it doesn't bother me a-tall." But he said, "Now y'all get over on the other side of that string; don't y'all bother him, now. Y'all stand on the outside."

I must've had over two hundred a-sittin' down on the outside of them strings. But they was just all the way around me! Oh boy, I'll tell you, I wanted to stay up there for two more days.

Ethel: *[Jimmie Lee's wife] He didn't want to come home.*

Jimmy Lee: *Yeah, I wanted to come home, but, you know, the man who had the money to go all the way through there, he could see somethin' good. Some of 'em shoutin', some of 'em prayin', some of 'em dancing. Man, you could see everything up there. Some of 'em got one leg, some of 'em got nary a leg. There was a lot of people blind, you know; they got to go just like I did.*

There was a one-legged man in Washington. He could play a French harp, and I beat him! He said, "Awww, he's from the South; he can't play nothin'!" By golly, I beat him!

Then I saw the parade, you know, and some people wadin' across that government place there, you know, the pond going down to the mansion where that five dollar bill is, you know [referring to the Lincoln Memorial depicted on the five dollar bill].

That street, you know, the one where the Government's mansion is? That's the one the President finally come out of. The Secretary of the White House come out, and the Secretary got me on that little ol' cart and run me all around the White House and down through the valley and brought me back. And they were still takin' pictures of it. Boy, it was somethin' to see.

Oh, and the Soul Train, oooh! I seen everybody! Miss Minnie Pearl passed. I said, "Howdee!" She said, "Howdee!" Tell you what, but I enjoyed myself.

But I'm the only one that went there for any drawing. They showed what they can make, you know. Like the man that made music out of bucket glass; he had different glasses. He hit this, and this one over here, and he had so much water in every one.

And that thing sounded like a guitar. Boy, I had never seen that before. I don't know how he done that! He could make it sing a tune: doon, doon, doon, doon, doon. See, he had one filled up a little higher than the other'n. I learnt that while I was over there.

Jimmy Lee plays his harp for you, simulating his Smithsonian performance. He plays a number about a dog chasing a fox, and you can really hear which one is which. Moreover, the hunter calls to the dog. Jimmy Lee talks to his harp—dramatizing or commenting on a scene—without missing a beat of the music. While the performance is in session, Ethel vies for your attention in conversation. You train the tape recorder mike on Jimmy Lee's music and turn toward her yourself.

Ethel hasn't much cared for the idea of being tape recorded. Earlier you had offered to turn the machine off if it made her uncomfortable. But she said, *That's all right. You get Jim.* Satisfied that you were following instructions, she remained in the room during the entire interview. Now she proudly shows you her scrapbook, while her husband is playing "Lost John" followed by "Icewater Blues."

Jimmy Lee: *I tell you the truth, I had fun. I didn't get drunk, I just took a little taste of beer till I was feelin' pretty good.* Ethel: *Oh, you did, you did, you did, too. I put his money between his socks, you know. And I said, "Now don't let nobody know what you got. Well the guy got high and called me on the telephone and said, "I got fifty-seven dollars in my pocket right now!" I hung up on him. [You all laugh].* Jimmy Lee: *She done hung up on me. I called her back again tomorrow [meaning the next day]. I got that money on stage playin'. I was playin' "I'll Fly Away." Well, we was goin' loud. We had a speaker over yonder, one down on the President's building and one up at the White House up there. And all those people come out. I come out famous in Washington; boy, I'm tellin you.*

The money thrown onto the stage while Jimmy Lee was "blowin' " his harp [like Ma Rainey II's fruit jar—in the chapter For the Seasoned Folklore Collector] seems to belong to the traditional practice among street musicians of passing the hat—another subject for folklore collectors to investigate.

Ethel begins to sing. Jimmy Lee offers to play his harp for accompaniment. *No, I don't want your harp.* She makes that definite. Ethel sings in a rich mellow contralto voice. By the third line of verse one, Jimmy Lee, who could no more remain silent than keep his own heart from beating, joins in—singing. Following orders, he does not play his harp. It is obvious that the two voices have had a lot of practice blending:

> *Some glad morning,*
> *When my life is o'er,*
> *I'll fly away.*
> *To a home on*
> *God's elected shore,*
> *I'll fly away.*

Jimmy Lee adds syncopation in counterpoint to Ethel's even, sustained notes:

> *I'll fly away, oh glory,*
> *I'll [fly away] fly away [in the morning].*
> *When I die, hallelujah, by and by*
> *I'll [fly away] fly away.*

Ethel, who still has her scrapbook open, gives you a small photograph of Dennis Wilson, the nephew whom Ethel and Jimmy Lee had been bringing up. *That boy followed me everywhere,* says Jimmy Lee. Twelve-year-old Dennis had also loved to watch Jimmy Lee paint. His uncle was teaching him how so the youngster could follow in the older man's footsteps one day. The pain of losing their boy never quite leaves them. The well-known situation of the country boy's attraction to that forbidden swimming hole on a sultry day too often meets with the outcome already dreaded by those who withhold their permission. Ethel hasn't been feeling well since it happened in '74, though she and Jimmy Lee both find solace in their religious faith.

Ethel hands you a photo clipping from between the pages of her scrapbook. You recognize the Reverend Ike. "I've seen him on TV," you say.

Jimmy Lee: *He's good; he's lovely. I'll tell you, he's really good.*
Ethel: *My boss lady saw his picture one day and said, "Here's Money Man!"*
Jimmy Lee: *I tell you, he can heal. He can heal the people. Ethel, she got a niece that's a healer. But I ain't got it that strong. Not to heal, I can't heal.*

Interviewer: Yeah, but you've made a lot of people happy.
Jimmy Lee: *That's exactly right.*
Interviewer: That's good for their health, too.
Jimmy Lee: *That's what I'd rather do. Make people happy.*

That reminds Jimmy Lee of the good times late at night, where the Southern folk musicians, all put up at the same hotel, would get together over a few "pops" as Jimmy Lee calls fermented beverages, and they'd "jam"—play together informally. *We'd make up riddles and talk riddles and things like that, you know.*
Interviewer: Can you remember any of those riddles? That interests me, 'cause I collect those.'
Jimmy Lee: *I can't hardly remember what* they *told, but I can remember mine. I told one about:*

> *One time the mackerel didn't go to stay.*
> *Horse took a big head and stayed all day.*
> *Wouldn't mind my kin folk; wouldn't mind my cousin.*
> *Wouldn't kiss a pretty girl at ten cents a dozen.*
> *The rain come wet me, the sun come dry me.*
> *Stand back, pretty girl, and don't you deny me!*

Ha, ha, ha, ha, ha, ha, ha, ha! We had all them riddles.
You ask Jimmy Lee to repeat the riddle one more time, so you'll be sure to get it down right, and you get a bonus:

> *When I was a little boy, lived by myself.*
> *All the bread and cheese, I had to lay them on the shelf.*
> *The rats and the mice cut fifty slice.*
> *I had to go to Baltimore to buy me a wife.*
> *The roads so muddy, the streets so narrow [pronounced to*
>   *rhyme with "car'uh"]*
> *I had to bring her back in a old wheelbarrow.*
> *The wheelbarrow broke and the wife had a fall.*
> *[In a hushed tone] The devil got the wheelbarrow and the*
>   *wife and all.*

Jimmy Lee takes his harp back out of his overalls pocket and plays "Pop Goes the Weasel" just for fun and then launches into serious renditions of "Out Beyond the Sun" and "Rock of Ages." While he plays, you both start out the door to go walking, because you've wanted Jimmy Lee to show you where he gets the clay he uses for his paintings. Ethel, who isn't feeling well, stays behind near the warmth of her woodburning bedroom heater [despite the eighty-degree spring day].

His front yard is filled with his latest paintings, propped up against large rocks or embankments, some in tiers, some on the ground in a circle. A dozen or more paintings of log houses. One of a water mill, which he especially wants you to admire. It is easy to comply.

He has painted the side of his own house to look as though it were faced with stone instead of concrete blocks. In the fine arts world, this technique would be called _trompe l'oeil_ or "fooling the eye."

Looks just like rock, don't it? That won't never come off.

"And the rain won't hurt it?" You ask with incredulity.

Nooo.

You guess not, reconsidering, not if the painting he left on an exterior wall in Washington, DC is still intact.

Now, I'm gonna build this up, and you can't tell it from rock, he declares, explaining that he intends to keep on, until the entire concrete base of his house is so decorated.

Still wielding tape recorder and camera, you follow Jimmy Lee through his garden, down an embankment, and across a plank which he has placed there to make it easier to get over a small stream and then up an embankment until you are walking the railroad tracks behind his house. Uncannily, Jimmy Lee knows just where to stop each time to move away the surface layer of Alabama clay with his hand and uncover very distinct shades ranging from burnt orange to purple.

With his finger he draws on a railroad tie, using some of the reds that he has uncovered nearby. _Lookit that. Look at how pretty that is. Now you got to put sugar in that before it will ever hold._ You recall how Jimmy Lee used the sorghum with mud in Washington: _Yeah. The man flew that sorghum mill up there; he flew it up there!_

While you are beginning to say your good-byes in his front yard, Jimmy Lee rubs another layer of green on a foliage scene, using a handful of Bermuda grass. You depart with a painting of a covered well done in black, white, and grays [shoe polish, flour, burnt matchsticks] and two cannas that promise to bloom bright red, for transplanting from his garden to yours. You are careful not to thank him directly for the plants [It's bad luck, remember?], but you tell him how beautiful they will look. Ethel and Jimmy Lee are both vigorous with their invitations for a return visit soon. Your heart is even fuller than your gift-laden arms.

Lida Holley, Primitive

Jimmy Lee's personal life is rooted in folk culture. His guileless, unsophisticated verbal expression belies a complexity of artistic genius. In the languages of clay and notes, he articulates an internalized sense of Southern heritage, broad in scope, stated primarily through setting. The very medium is mud: landscapes, structures, artifacts, the featured subjects. And his musical virtuosity on a simple folk instrument is punctuated by environmental echoes of locomotives or baying hounds.

On another day, at another cheerful, bustling, colorful crafts fair—a little more than a hundred miles away from where you first met Jimmy Lee—you conduct a brief on-site interview with a verbally sophisticated, college educated Southern woman, whose personal life-style is obviously not primarily folk. She, however, paints her impressions of what might be Jimmy Lee's folk heritage. [It is hers by reason of observation and indirect experience.] Her emphasis is on people as subjects. She paints in acrylics, a sophisticated medium, in an unsophisticated style known to elite circles as "primitive."

There is always a good bit of "fine art" at a crafts show, much of it quite wonderful. But inasmuch as folk art is a collector's particular delight, you are drawn up short by an exhibit of canvasses which glow with unadulterated color.

A few moments later you are introducing yourself to a sprite of a woman, the artist Lida Holley, and her husband Ray. Between your curiosity and her effervescence it is difficult to tell who is interviewing whom. In less than an hour, with the informed assurance of one who has practically watched you grow up, Lida is introducing

Marshal Hagler

Lida Holley paints in acrylics, a sophisticated medium, in an unsophisticated style known to elite circles as "primitive."

you to old friends, who are dropping by to see her latest paintings. Here's how your end of it goes.

Interviewer: You said you've been painting for five years. Tell me how you got started?
Lida Holley: *It'll be five years in October. My daughter was teaching art, giving private lessons. And she said, "Mama,*

come and take art in my class." I said, "Ooh, I don't want to."
She finished in art, and I sure didn't want to take up my time
with art. But I went 'cause she made me.

About the fourth lesson, she sat me in the corner, and she
said, "You can't take it with the class." So she called one of her
professors from Auburn University and he came over. She said,
"I think Mama is a 'primitive.' " And I said, "Is that good or
bad?"

They said, "It's good." They jumped up and down and
carried on. And from then, the first show I went to, I sold four
hundred dollars' worth, which to me was a fortune.

Interviewer: What are your media? What kind of materials do you like to use?

Lida: *I paint in acrylics.*

Interviewer: Is that what you started with, right away?

Lida: *I've never done anything but acrylics. My daughter said I can't do all of them. She won't let me. She said, "No, Mama, you can't." So, now I've been to California, New York; I've just been all over the United States now.*

Interviewer: Have you taught anybody else?

Lida: *You can't teach anybody how to be primitive. You have to be a born primitive. And they tell me there are not but about four in the United States. I don't know. I don't have any idea. There's that colored woman in New Orleans, Christina Hunter, who's up in her eighties. She's a primitive. ·They say you can't teach anybody, and, if you're not a primitive, that's just it, so I don't know.*

Interviewer: What was the subject of the first thing that you painted that made your daughter sit up and take notice?

Lida: *Well, it was some cups. She put a still life of some cups up there, and I couldn't hang the cups. I couldn't set them down, and I couldn't take them up. They were just floating around, the funniest thing! She said the coloring was beautiful, she loved the coloring.*

So then the next thing was she posed for a portrait. And I did her, and she turned out to be black, and not white like she is. I don't know why I did that [laughing]; I sure don't. So, I was just a real funny artist. I've had loads of fun.

Marshal Hagler

Flower Arrangement by Lida Holley

Interviewer: I think that's what it should be.
Lida: *And we just go to shows all the time. I just don't price them high. But they like those little five-dollar paintings. I sold*

*out yesterday afternoon and had to go home and paint some
more last night.*
Mr. Holley: *She never had a lesson.*
Lida: *When they first told me what* primitive *means, they said
"untutored." That wasn't the word they used. They said "uneducated," that's it. I* am *educated. I've been to college. They
said, "That's not what we mean. It means 'uneducated in what
you're doing.' "*
Interviewer: Well, congratulations. Isn't it nice to get a new lease on
life at any time? I hope you're not embarrassed if I ask you your age.
You don't have to tell me.
Lida: *I don't care. I'm sixty-five. We've had something so
wonderful: We've had our first grandchild.*

Your conversation is temporarily interrupted by sales. When
conducting interviews at a fair, you make a point of urging the
person who has given you permission to tape to feel free to take care
of any customers. Fun is primary, but it is not the sole objective.
Craftspeople do attend to sell their wares. Breaks in the taping
procedure afford good opportunities to shoot film or to think up
questions that the spontaneity of the situation might not otherwise
have permitted.

You've been getting acquainted with Mr. Holley. Lida returns to
hand you a brochure containing the reproduction of one of her
larger portraits.

Lida: *My daughter won't let me sell it. She has put back so many
of my things and won't let me sell them at all. Mr. W_____,
head of the Art Department, came [to the exhibit] and—what do
you call it when you criticize shows? Well, you know what I'm
talking about. He got to that painting and he looked at it and
says, "Golly, what color!" And then he stopped. He said,
"Golly, anybody had guts enough to put those colors in
there"—It's the brightest picture I've ever painted, yet.*

*Let me tell you what happened at a school I was invited to
visit. I asked all the pupils to write what they liked best about
Calico Fort [arts fair]. And one little girl wrote, "I like the lady
who paints like me best."*

Lida points to some miniature versions of the largest canvasses, depicting similar Southern rural scenes teeming with images of black folklife.

I sold two for ten dollars each yesterday, and then I thought, "No, I don't think I'll do any more because it just takes too much time. So I'll stick to something that won't take time, like Mammies, little boys fishing, and all that."

"I'm not doing too many flowers now," reports Lida, "I'm too busy trying to preserve what we have *seen all our life* out in the country."

I did that this morning about six o'clock. [In a confidential tone] You know, you can paint fast if you're a primitive!

One time, I painted a little boy, and I left his eyes out. A lady called me up the next day and said, "Oh Lida, you left the eyes out! Can I bring it by and let you put the eyes in?" I said, "No, he blind." They've all got little stories to them.

Well, I had one little girl [on a painting], and she's all dressed up like she's going somewhere. Everybody else has on every-

day clothes, but she's all mixed up on the time. She thought it was Sunday. But it's not; it's Saturday.

And that's a cat. You might think it was something else.
Interviewer: No, I had no doubt at all.
Lida: *The kittens, they look like rabbits.*
Interviewer: They look happy; I can tell that.
Lida: *Everything I do is happy in the pictures.*

Johnny Shines, Gut Bucket Bluesman

The realization of her own talent, discovered by experts who had to convince her of its validity, is still new to Lida Holley. She has yet to break it in until she can wear it as comfortably as an old pair of shoes—without having to think about how it feels. On the other hand, Jimmy Lee's harmony with circumstance, however acquired, is not owing to a lack of painful experiences.

Secure in his considerable talent, bluesman Johnny Shines, who has traveled this country from coast to coast along with half a hundred foreign nations, has received an experiential education in a restless world—the context for his struggle toward inner integrity. Johnny perceives his art from either of two directions: from within his own cultural sphere, as an uncontestable legacy; but, more objectively, as a tradition that requires validation, especially to the turned backs of some of his own people.

He lives in your hometown. You've met him at folk arts festivals and attended a number of his concerts. His name is in the phone book. You take the initiative and call to make an appointment to really talk about the blues and Johnny Shines.

The facts that Johnny Shines has had a number of references made to him in books about the folk blues, has cut half a dozen albums on which he solos, and has had at least one article and one chapter in a book on blues devoted to him seem only to have whetted his eagerness to share his feelings about his art.

The day is a scorcher. Johnny's tidy house sits on a bright green lawn in a well-populated residential neighborhood, but there are open areas out back, where folks have vegetable gardens.

I just come out of the field, Johnny explains as you drive up. *Out there plantin' peas, and boy, I've had it.* His speech lacks

John Earl

Bluesman Johnny Shines among friends

Alabama sounds. You already know he was born in Memphis, but you think you detect a good dose of the Midwest in his voice. Johnny did live and perform in Chicago for a number of years. He left because, *For one thing, I was fed up with the rat race.*

And the next thing, my daughter [his only child] died and left ten kids. And I had seven of those ten kids. Unable to get a loan and buy a house on the west side of Chicago, he brought his suddenly acquired second family of seven children to Alabama. *They've thinned out now, and it's about time, 'cause my nerves is not as good as they once was. Like the old song, "The old gray mare ain't what she used to be."* Johnny is sixty-three.

He modulates his voice, even in conversation, like an orator. *I come from the South, and I want to elevate myself. And so I went to study music. But there were so many things that I was doing right, before I started taking music, that I found out was wrong, after I started taking music, that I had to go back and get right. Well, I was a much better musician before. But as a technician, it improved my techniques. But as a musician, it was a handicap.*

I can teach you how to play, but I cannot teach you how to feel. When you feel it, other people can feel you; if you're a mechanical man, who feels a mechanical man? When you're loose, doing things that you feel good over doing, your audience is with you; once ever the spell is with you, it's the same spell that you cast upon your audience.

It's just like a preacher. He might be a very good speaker— you understand what I mean?—and not know anything about the Bible at all, only what somebody sits down and reads to him the night before. And he gets up the next morning and preach it, you understand what I mean? But now there are lots of things that come to him during his sermon, you know, which he's just adding in, that you'll find out nine times out of ten is right, you know? It belongs there—something that other preachers do not explain to the people because they're a handicap to them, you see, and they enjoys those Cadillacs, you know.

And through his liberation, this poor, ignorant preacher, who drives a raggedy car—and is gonna end up on a jackass yet—brings out more on a subject than a well-read preacher. He say, "God sent me to preach. He didn't tell me to half preach. That's what I have to do." But he don't have the largest congregation, you know what I mean? And lots of things he bring out, people takes offense with. But it is to be spoken [The voice is stentorian]. And if it hurts, it just have to hurt—but it look like he's the one that's hurtin'.

You understand the parable. You've seen fans go up to Johnny and say, "You're so talented; you sing and play better than most of 'em. Why haven't you made it big like, say, B. B. King?" Even though it looks as if Johnny's hurting, you understand that he's got to do his "thing" like that poor preacher.

B. B. King, he come to Memphis. There was all of us there in Memphis. But now here's the thing about it. If they told B. B., "We're going to pay you three dollars a day," or if they told him, "We're going to pay you three hundred," it was still all right.

I've seen things happen to him that couldn't have happened to me! I couldn't have beared it, you understand what I mean?

Hoping he'll elucidate, you tell him how impressed you were by his recent on-stage observation during a concert, "The blues are a prayer." His response, more than you expected, is both a sermon from the heart and a folk history of the blues:

The blues is an English version of field hollers which was credited to the slaves, which was really their prayer. You see, the blues have been described as lots of folly and foolishness, and jolly music—people having a lot of fun.

Back in slavery time, the field hands, they wasn't allowed, for a long time, to attend church or have prayer meetings. And so many of the women—if she didn't have a child by the time she was thirty years old, she was put in the log field alongside her brother and her father. But, if a field hand couldn't pick so many hundred pounds of cotton a day, and if he disobeyed orders, he got a whipping. How could these things as they have been described to us and to the world—how could this be folly?

When the white man's relatives and friends come to the South to visit, they'd hear these people in sad tones of voices late in the evening when the dew was falling, the echo drifting across the fields and meadows, and they heard these people crying out. And down in the fields the hands was carryin' on this chirping and chattering, and moaning and groaning—you understand what I mean—what's supposed to be happy. They didn't expect to find them with uplifted faces towards the sky and some shouting out, some mumbling, and some, their lips was just working.

And they started asking questions about the sadness of these people. That's when the overseers told the black preachers, "Now you must stop them hands from singin' them 'reals,'" meaning "reality." They had English overseers, they had German overseers; some were Swedish, some were Irish, and probably some Polish—all speaking in different accents, you understand what I mean? And naturally they [the overseers] didn't learn the language very fast.

In their own tongue, they could stand under the master's feet and talk about him and sing about him—you understand what I mean—and make plans and send messages to other plantations, and he didn't know what they were talking about. And when he found out that this was going on also, he really shook down on them.

So they had to sing about "walking to Jerusalem just like John," "I be so glad when I get over," and stuff like that. And that's how these songs came in, which we now call "gospel songs," "spiritual songs," "Doctor Watson songs." They came out of the same people which we call "slaves." Before, they was called "reals." Later on, they were called "blues."

The average man now don't realize how the jazz come out of the blues. The blues is the original American music. All of American music come out of the bowels of the blues.

When these blues first originated, the people played these guitars; they didn't know how to play them in the tunings they're playing them in now. They played them in open keys. And that was with slides. Most of us think of slides as something new, but slides is just as old as slavery time. The bottleneck slide was most original.

They had to learn to play the guitar in any way that they could. And they did these open tunings because they didn't know how to make G, D, E, A, C—you understand what I mean? So they used a slide to make these chords, not knowing the names of these chords.

I love the Rolling Stones, and when Jimi Hendrix played "Rock Me Baby" and "Red House," those songs may be considered blues by some folks, but they're not the real blues. See, when you sing about "you got beautiful legs, you got beautiful eyes, hair like an angel," you know, it's really a love song.

The blues is a story, and if you don't hear the story and don't understand the story, you really don't know the song. You see, blues come into every respect of life. To my way of thinkin' blues is really a story within itself which is describing experience.

Muddy Waters—years ago you would have known him as a farmer, the guy you send the money to or don't even send any money to, to come in and play on a Saturday night party. I used to play for a dollar a night and all the whiskey I could drink. Mostly road houses out in the country. Jukes and things like that—Saturday night fish fries. It's not that long ago. Charlie Patton and all those guys. People was never interested in those people until folklorists began to come in and weed those people out.

You comment upon Johnny's having been friends with the well-known bluesman Robert Johnson: "I'll bet everybody wants to know about Robert Johnson from you. Now there's a man who became a legend. The fact that there's a mystery about the way he died has a way of catching the imagination."

No one really knows [how he died]. Well, I really think myself that he died of ulcers. He drank very heavy and being a musician, going from place to place, eatin' all types of food, all hours, no regularity. He probably didn't have sense enough to notice ulcers was killin' him.

Now Robert Johnson's type of blues music is the way back, down home blues, you know. Gut bucket blues. It wasn't the update, the shoutin' kind of blues that we've finally come into. He was pretty gutty. And Charlie Patton was kind of a gutty type, only he played an upper tempo. But he was very good because he had kind of a gravel voice, you know, and he was very down home.

He didn't make chords and changes and do things regular. You couldn't call it a "twelve-bar" blues. It was just his blues, you know. He changed it anytime he felt like it. He turned it back anytime he felt like it. He went for the bridge anytime he felt like it. Then it wasn't bridge stuff, you know. You just played and sang, you know. Any place you started up on, that was what was ended up on. And we called it "gut bucket blues."

Well, now we have blues that have bridge to it, you know, and different ones takin' solos. There's room for it all. I don't condemn any of it. Thing about it is the description. I think you should describe these things as they are.

The blues are dyin', but they could be brought back over-night. They could be the hottest thing on the market. You see,

"I can teach you how to play, but I cannot teach you how to feel."

you can make anybody or anything you want if you've got the radio, newspapers, and TV with you.

Johnny writes his own songs. In order to keep from drawing on anyone else's material, even inadvertently, he explains, *I can't tell you anything that's on the radio. I listen to the radio, but I don't hear. But you can't write anyway without writing other people's music. As the Bible says, "There is nothing new; what is to be has been." But let it be your own version in your own way.*

You remind Johnny about a concern you've heard him voice before: "It's interesting to me that you find so many white folks who love this material, while—as you've told me yourself—most young blacks won't have anything to do with it."

That's right. That's right. The average young blacks really don't want to relive this history in memory. He wants to get away from it and forget it. Wherein the white boys and girls find it very tantalizing. It makes them think. What we all need to do is think. I think it's so bad to forget the past, because when you forget the past, you're automatically out of focus for the future.

You ask Johnny to quote the lyrics which he thinks are most characteristic of his own blues. He precedes them with a recollection from the old days when he was playing mainly in the Southeast:

Here's this little white boy, hauntin' the hell out of us. As soon as you'd put the tub down, he'd grab it and try to play it. He'd change the tuning on it. He was really a pest. But he was trying to do something. He did it!

He learned to play all of my tunes. He learned to play all of Robert Junior's tunes. And then he went back and he dug up Robert Johnson, which is Robert Junior's stepfather. He learned to do his tunes.

He sings black songs and plays black music like black people. And he's as white as any white man I ever seen in my life. Now I loved him. But when Columbia taken him over, he cracked up. He blew his wig.

I met him in Ann Arbor, and he had one of my albums under his arm. And he still could open his arms, you know, and I went to him. He filled up my arms, you know, and cried like a baby.

"What's wrong?"

He says, "I didn't do it, I didn't do it, I didn't do it, I didn't do it."
I says, "I don't follow you man."
He said, "I feel like you should have gotten it." He said, "It was just dumped in my lap."
I told him, "I would have taken it just like you did. One hundred twenty-six thousand a year for five years, who wouldn't have taken it?"

His eyes twinkle as he confides the real answer to the rhetorical question in his reminiscence: *Maybe a fool like me.* And those lyrics?

> *I don't do the Chubby Checker,*
> *James Brown, or no one else,*
> *Because the good Lord made us all,*
> *And me, I just be myself.*

I think I was playing for the public before B. B. King. But now he's become very famous, very famous. Why should I want to be B. B. King?

If true humility is a quality that can only be possessed unawares, what you're feeling on your way out of Johnny Shines' home must be a close approximation. It is humbling to be a folklore collector—to experience such undemanding generosity and hospitality from folks who not only open up their homes to you but their very minds.

In turn, folklore collecting seems to bring out more and more small acts of thoughtfulness in you. You start picking up your telephone more regularly just to say hello to an informant who may be shut in. You follow up some of your interview-visits with notes of thanks.

You develop a habit of bringing a little something along when you go to the home of a resource person—some fruit, perhaps a box of doughnuts or a homemade cake, a six-pack if appropriate. You're a little more concerned than ever before not to take inadvertent advantage of those less able to pay power bills or buy groceries than you. And still you feel humble just to be where you are.

You run your tape recorder on batteries, even when the wall socket is handy in the interviewing room. And sometimes you decline the offer of a meal, though only if you feel certain that your host will not take offense. And you have a glass of ice-water or a cola instead of dinner—perhaps stretching the truth a bit in saying that you just finished a meal before coming over.

For the Seasoned Folklore Collector

You've glimpsed the diversity in unity and the grand in the familiar. Your respect for the unassuming ingenuity of the folk is second nature now, but you never cease to be amazed at the sheer abundance of grassroots talents.

You're gaining confidence; you're ready to go that extra mile to collect folklore, to become involved in projects which take you farther afield than the other side of the fence.

Down the road from your own backyard, you might find yourself collecting lore from artists in residence at a folklife center in the Ozarks—a year-round living museum and fair combined. Or, you might find yourself tape recording a conversation with a traditional blues singer at her apartment before you drive her to work at a downtown Memphis nightspot. There you spend the rest of the evening enjoying her performance and those of an entire band of old-timers from the days when Beale Street used to reverberate with the sounds you're hearing again tonight.

You may even turn folklore sleuth by tracking a legend down several roads, discovering along the way your ability to synthesize data, appreciate the mysterious, and sympathize with the macabre. It is then you notice that folklore, which has taught you more about life than you ever expected to learn from it, has just come full circle to teach you a lesson that improves your outlook even on death and decay.

Folk Center

If you visit one of our nations's few folk centers situated in a state park, you can enjoy all the benefits of an outdoor vacation, as well as a folklore collector's holiday bonanza. At the Ozark Folk Center in Mountain View, Arkansas, for example, you may reap a great deal of information about traditional crafts. Talking to the folks at such a demonstration center, you are likely to gain some indelible impressions of the regional sensibilities of folks down the road from you—of their sense of place. You also might encounter folks who have chosen alternative life-styles for themselves by returning to grassroots occupations. Each in his or her own way speaks of "just a feeling that I had to express."

Basketry with the Stewarts: Jackie Stewart is originally from Harrison. He says, *I moved down here my senior year in high school. Janet's from here, born and raised here.* Though they learned their craft together, Janet had been exposed to it longer than her husband. She concedes:

I'm familiar with the craft except, well, when you're from around here, it's not as important until you're not from around here, if you know what I mean. If you grow up with it, it's just so boring.

I met Jackie, and he got this wild idea that he needed to join the Marine Corps; and so we stayed at Camp Lejeune in North Carolina for two years. We came back; and I realized, you know, that it wasn't all trash. Five or six years ago, I wouldn't have ever dreamed that I would be doing this and enjoying it.

Janet is working on a weed basket. The next few questions are for Jackie, who has stopped weaving to split wood. At what time of the year do you prefer to harvest your white oak? And what kind of terrain do the best trees come from?

The tree keeps its moisture better in the winter. In the summer, when the sap is up, the sap will dry out quicker. The sun will draw the sap out a lot quicker than in the wintertime. During the winter, I take them from everywhere.

During the summertime, I take them strictly from an old

Marshal Hagler

Janet Stewart adds on the odd split to a weed basket intended to hold dried flowers.

hillside; an old hillside works better than anywhere else. In the wintertime, it don't matter. During the winter, I use a saw all the time. Cut them as big as I can get. During the summer, I got about like a ten-inch tree. I like the wintertime better; I can get a bigger tree.

Do you have any reservations about sap edges?

If the heart's good, I use the edges. I just use what I can. I try to use it all.

About how long will the supply of wood you try to harvest at once last you?

I try to use it up in about two weeks. I don't try to get no more than two weeks'. In the summertime, it dries out; in the wintertime, we don't work no longer than two weeks outside.

Do you care about the temperature of that water? (The reference is to a metal tub in which white oak splits are soaking.)

I like it warm. It can get pretty annoying. This last winter, at our workshop, the wind blew our insulation down; and this tub

Jackie Stewart uses a froe to split a length of white oak. He will repeat the process over and over until the strips of wood are as thin and pliable as those hanging on the nearby wall.

of water would freeze up. We didn't do a whole lot of work this winter at all, except a little in the living room.

If I was faster, I could get rich at it [making baskets]. During the winter, I lose all that I made because I'm still not a vet. A family by the name of G_____ does it, and they can do ten baskets a day of any size they want to per person. There's a whole slew of them there.

Don G_____'s a fourth generation basket maker, and he's been doing it since he was big enough; and he's thirty-three now. They waste no time at all. They're fine basket makers. Someday, we'll be able to do that, too. Two different times we've averaged eight a day, completely, start to finish, and that's in two years.

You ask Janet if the cone-shaped device she is using is a mold. She explains:

What I want is eight different sides, right? OK, I have four long uprights, we call them. You put them on this simply to help hold. So, this is just a stand. We call it a weed basket stand, you know, and I'll just weave so far down while the basket is on there till I think the basket's going to hold together when I let go of it.

And what I'm going to do right now is try to get the widest [split] and cut it in two. Then I can have an odd number of splits

Jackie and Janet Stewart have chosen white oak split basket making as their full-time vocation. To them it's an art.

so I can get my over-and-under weaving going. Because, if you have an even number, it will go over the same way [instead of alternating].

Jackie: *The handle is just stuck down between the weavers and the uprights, and the hoop holds it on. The hoop is laced to the weavers. It works like a Chinese finger puzzle. The harder you pull on it, the tighter it holds.*

Interviewer: Do you enjoy doing any chair-bottom weaving?

Jackie: *Yeah. I can do three a night goin' and comin'. That's a craft that my Grandpa taught me there. He showed me how to do chair bottoms when I was about nine years old. I did a couple and forgot it. About two years ago I started doing it again.*

I'd rather do baskets, but there's not as much money in them. Chairs are just quick money for me. I can do it so fast, I kinda feel like I'm a machine.

Do you ever make baskets out of any other material than white oak?

We'll use flat split reed. I think it's good practice on weaving. Whenever I'm experimenting with a new size, I use the reed. We're trying to stick strictly to white oak, though. Trying to make a living from it.

It's hard on the hands, isn't it? You can get all kinds of cuts.

That's really your own fault if you let your knife get dull and then cut yourself. Every time my knife gets dull, I end up cutting myself. You get very few splinters; and by using the water, it keeps your hands from getting callused up and swelling shut on you.

Last summer we did a few just completely green and in about two weeks, our hands were getting so stiff we couldn't do nothing at all with them. We're musicians, too, and we count on our music of a nighttime to bring in a little more income. I play a banjo, and Janet plays a guitar. We play up here in the auditorium. Last year we played with two different fiddlers. This year we play with an old fiddler named Morrison.

Janet: *By ourselves some, too. Our little girl—she'll be two in June—she dances at night. She'll wear little long dresses. She*

just gets up there dancing away, and she just stomps her feet.
Jackie: *She's been raised here.*

Clarice Chitwood, native weaver: Clarice Chitwood earns her living at a traditional loom. Her craft requires much patience, of which she happens to have plenty.

Basically, it's very simple. But it takes a little while to learn, I'll put it that way.

Now this is fairly coarse thread that I'm using here for a work thread. You know, you might at times be using thread that's much finer, and you'd have to have twice as many. But, you know, it takes me about half a day to set this up like it is here. You can see what it might take if you were weaving full length and if you were using finer thread.

"Anything that you carry your thread on would be a shuttle," Clarice Chitwood points out. "This one is a homemade variety. Someone asked me one day, 'What kind of wood is your shuttle made of?' And I said, 'I think it's a side off an apple box, when they used to pack apples in boxes.' "

It's so very simple. You pick up any number of threads you want, but in this case, I picked up four, and two over two. See what I mean? It's called interweave, but that's the way it's done.

Do the foot levers have special names?

Well, we call them pedals; and you might have them numbered like 1, 2, 3, 4, and you know, like that.

The reed, or dent, is what takes care of your threads per inch. This is called a twelve-dent reed that I have in here, and that's what it means—twelve threads per inch. If you were using finer thread, you might put two through there, you see. That would make twenty-four.

To the question, "Is weaving traditional in your family?" Mrs. Chitwood replies, *No closer than my grandmother, my father's mother. My mother did beautiful handwork, but I never saw her weave. It's one of those things that intrigued me, and I was determined to learn how to do it. It's self-taught.*

I've been here for six years, I guess. I was born not too far from here, in the county. Now, I have been away. People tell me I don't speak like people here, but I am a native.

Do you ever weave yardage for clothing?

Well, I have woven a little yardage for myself, but I wouldn't want to undertake it for long. It's a little bit hard to handle the handwoven. If you laid a pattern down and tried to cut that, if you weren't very careful, it's going to pull out.

How was it done in former times?

If you'll look at their clothing, they were simple, straight lines that didn't require a lot of cutting.

When you thank her for allowing you to interrupt her work, Mrs. Chitwood replies, *I don't mind. But there has been an instance or two when people were very impolite. It made me feel like this: Well, they're just a bunch of ignorant hillbillies, and they don't know what it's all about anyhow.*

That's like gettin' old, exclaims a woman standing next to you in the workshop. *People sometimes think they have to help you along, and you don't want to be helped!*

Right. It just gives me a feeling that I don't like. I don't know how well you know mountain people. They have a tremendous amount of, rightly or wrongly, pride. Sometimes it stumbles me.

I can remember being a wife somewhere else. And I hesitated when people said, "Where are you from?" to say "Arkansas," because Arkansas was such a backward, you know, sort of a place, that you hesitated. But I'm very proud and I'm glad.

Our ancestors, the people who were here before we were, they were certainly clever people. They were ingenious. They were hard-working people, or they couldn't have survived.

David Matthews' mettle: David Matthews stumbled into traditional blacksmithing by the back door. Once inside, he developed the conscientious point of view of a "periodist," as he calls it:

I've had disappointed craftspeople come through before, expecting to see an old blacksmith at the Center rather than a young blacksmith. I can understand that.

"But," you protest, "there is something to be said for the young blacksmith who cares enough to do what you're trying to accomplish."

Actually, I was a little shocked that they would let me in here. I just happened in at the right time. I was really curious and always standing around and asking questions. They didn't know I'd be any good. They just needed somebody to be in here when the regular blacksmith left. It was lucky for me, because it subsidized me to learn the craft.

At the Folk Center, David has a place to work and is in the process of teaching himself traditional smithing skills:

I'm trying to avoid painting. Now, that's an attempt to get back to the original. The oil finish is so much better. You have to heat it. The best way is in a two-hundred- or three-hundred-degree fire, and it'll burn the excess off the metal and help that oil to soak into the pores. The metal's in focus, so you can see all the handle marks and everything.

David wishes he could practice his folk craft in an authentically restored community environment but is aware of potential drawbacks as well:

When I first heard about the Folk Center, I thought it was set up more or less like a village, you know, with regular village

Marshal Hagler

"My father was an aerospace engineer. I've completely transcended all the pressure put on me to become a pharmacist or something else, to do what I want to do." For David Matthews that's traditional blacksmithing.

shops. But I like the low-key atmosphere here, the way people can ramble through and stop and stay and talk for a long time.

You know, some of the log cabins we built out here. I really got into keeping the notches from being cut out with a chain saw. I was willing to do the work by hand. They couldn't understand why I wanted to work harder than I needed to.

The old blacksmith's shops—very few people realize that the ones that really made history were operated by water wheels. They had big tall handles, you know, big huge log beams operated by wheels that went up and down to work that metal.

The old man who works in the shop has shown me different things, some of which I have rejected, trying to get closer to the true sense of the craft. For instance, a froe—a shingle splitting tool, he made it out of car springs. That's kind of the way blacksmiths in the last twenty or thirty years made them. The old-time froes were made out of wrought iron that was much thicker. With a trip hammer, I would be able to work that heavier metal and to make a froe, and even to handweld it in the fire.

But, I'm a living example of somebody that stuck it out and managed to survive out here, you know, and have changed my life. I meet a lot of people who are trying to get away from where they grew up and what they're doing now. I just thought, at first, somebody more authentic would fill the bill better than I.

Reagan Cole on this, that, and the dulcimer: Demonstrating folk artists are not the only people the folklore collector encounters down the road. It can be pleasant and informative to strike up conversations with fellow tradition lovers who, like you, are spectators or visitors at a folk event. Reagan Cole, engaged in conversation outside an auditorium where a mountain dulcimer contest had taken place, is a dulcimer maker back home. He is also a man with a wry sense of humor, some acute observations to share, and fluency in folk instruments.

People, I think, like instruments with flaws in them. It's organic. If you don't want any flaws in your tone, if you want a

Marshal Hagler

Reagan Cole displays two dulcimers which he has made. I'm interested in design. I've been making radical bends and strange shapes. I'm using a western red cedar here, and there's a big debate in guitar-making circles about whether it's ethical, because it starts out sounding like mellow old spruce."

consistent thing, you can set up a synthesizer to make any sound you want.

If you build several dulcimers exactly alike, each one of them will still be slightly different. I think I made a series of thirty of them that were identical. I did that one time. Now, I experiment a lot. I did one that had a Dutch tulip for a sound hole and a dogwood blossom on the head stock. I bend my wood freehand and don't use any molds.

I just did it as a hobby, and then I got involved in it. There's a certain charm to it. It's got everything you want. It's complicated enough that you can't become a total master of the art or craft. There're old traditions and there are new theories, and stuff like that. If Stradivari had known about American wood, he would have used it. They were just putting old boats in the ocean about that time.

Dulcimer *is a macaronic word. Macaronic words make no sense in any language. Like if you take our language, which is English, we had a lot of beautiful words that have all been covered up by Greek and Latin phrases. Vance Randolph's new book is full of a lot of those English words that people aren't allowed to use, whereas people are allowed to use the Greek and Latin—I looked up all the informants in the Eureka Springs area for Randolph's book; and I determined that they're all dead, which is why he published it.* Dulcis *is Latin and* melos *is Greek, so if you're a Greco-Roman from somewhere in the middle of the Mediterranean Sea, you'd understand the word.*

Some people can play better with three strings. Some people can play better with four strings. A girl at the contest had a courtin' dulcimer [built for two players]. She had both sides of it tuned to different scales; so when she came to a passage with a different tune, she simply turned the instrument around and played the other half.

Bluegrass is not Ozark music. Arkansas has produced a distinctive regional version of rock 'n roll that is fully as identifiable as anything that blew out of Texas. I was going through a record store in London, and I came across this record, "Arkansas Rock Pile." There's a jazz scene here; but all the principals have mainly gone away to New York, where they can make a living at it. That's home cooking, though. Those guys, their roots are here; their music is based on what they heard growing up, but when you get these guys coming around with all this secondhand Bill Monroe . . . .

I decided to go on vacation to see the world, and I ended up seeing Ireland and the middle of the North Sea for a while—oil rigs. I used my oil rig money to buy tools, made some rather crude dulcimers, and went out hawking them in the streets of Ireland.

When I was in Ireland, the people over there were brewing up a sort of homegrown version of bluegrass. Basically, you take the same old bunch of fiddle tunes that are spread all the way around the world, and you orchestrate it somehow. They've put together these Irish bands with Irish pipes, fiddle, penny whistle, flute, concertina, harp, you know, the cheap ones. It doesn't sound anything like bluegrass, but the spirit is about the same. I mean, Sean O'Riada is the Bill Monroe of Irish music—but Sean drank himself to death.

Reagan produces a penny whistle and plays in succession "Teetotaler's Reel," and "Dixie." The brass penny whistle, according to Reagan, *is the real thing, made in Sheffield, England. Three and a half dollars. I sell quite a few of these to tourists, you know. I can chase people out of the door of my shop with these.*

Reagan Cole performs a highly discernible "Turkey in the Straw" on Arkansas' indigenous instrument, the pickin' bow.

Pickin' bow lesson from Woodson Gannoway: Woodson Gannoway explains:

Your mouth changing the volume is what makes the pickin' bow work. I do a lot of the work in the back of my mouth with the arch in my tongue. But the volume in your mouth is what makes the sound you get or don't get. It may not look like my mouth is doing much when I play and change the sound, but that's because I've learned to do most of it inside.

Where you hold it may change the sound a little, because the bow vibrates. But basically, it's a noncritical instrument. It's simple. It's a piece of wood with a string on it. The string and the wood ought to match each other fairly well. And other than that, that's it.

Letting the tension off of it when you're not playing it is about all the care and feeding there is. Don't step on it, don't run over it with a truck; though you could probably get away with some of that. But, it's a noncritical instrument, and you're getting a lot of music out of a small instrument without much trouble to it. It's one of the best I know. So that's a pickin' bow.

I bring them up here as rough planks and finish them off during the folk festival. They sell a lot through the shops. I wholesale most of my stuff. I started about three years ago.

Marshal Hagler

Woodson Gannoway, who makes and sells Arkansas pickin' bows, recommends that "you kinda lay it across your cheek and put your lips against the back of it lightly. It doesn't have to have any pressure."

Before that I made baskets for five years. I'm in general woodworking and getting more into metal working—blacksmithing particularly.

I've always been doing stuff with my hands. I didn't grow up in this kind of environment. I grew up in Illinois. I didn't know anything about this kind of stuff until I was grown. But I was always doing something, making something. Leatherwork: I braided bullwhips for a long time. Just a feeling that I had to express.

As I learned that this was a part of me that sitting on wasn't going to get rid of, I learned to work it into my life more generally than I might have if I had continued to do the things that I grew up learning. I was trained in electronics and photography. I didn't find the work satisfying, so I stopped working in other fields. I started on stuff I knew absolutely nothing about. It worked out.

Marshal Hagler

Customers who purchase candles at this shop may dip their own, creating whatever colors and designs imaginations dictate. Only confirmed purists leave with their candles still white.

Marshal Hagler

Cindy Rice explains about candle making: "Each time I dip it, I add a layer of wax to it, a layer about as thin as a piece of paper."

Tracking A Legend

New roads can open up to the experienced folklorist who becomes interested in exploring legendry or a particular legend. You can record an interesting folktale and file it in your collection as a completed item, whether or not you ever hear another version of that particular tale or its theme. But you can never be quite certain that you've garnered all there is of a legend. With the possible exception of a body of family anecdotes, which circulates more narrowly, most types of legends cannot be swept up and tied in neat bundles.

Legends contain some kernels of hard fact, which may be researched, cautiously, with the aid of library materials or old newspapers, and by talking to folks who have relevant documents in their private possession. Yet legends are not factual reports. Narrative details from a single informant may vary in time. Moreover, details tend to vary, often considerably, from teller to teller. That is the nature of legendry.

Tracking a legend begins when you recognize a good story as having all the earmarks of an historical account except that much of what is allegedly true defies authentication. The process continues as you are able to collect variants which, in turn, confirm this quasi-historical account as folk narrative. For legends of any kind—supernatural, religious, historical, geographical, or heroic—are sincerely believed by the teller or by someone from whom the teller heard it.

Collecting legendry offers all the excitement of being an investigative reporter without the burden of having to discriminate between conflicting accounts. There is no mystery that has to be solved, only an intriguing story to enjoy. Armchair psychology and speculation about plot elements are part of the fun, so long as they are recognized for what they are: hypotheses, which may themselves be part of the body of narrative tradition.

Legends are migratory. Sources of information about a legend can range from informants in a single folk group or community to informants dispersed in several geographical areas, and to assorted types of documents as well. Collecting legendry thus becomes an intermittent but ongoing process of picking up loose ends and digging for bits and pieces.

The legend of Hazel Farris is a type of "personal" legend, so termed because it centers on a particular person. Like most legends, it contains sensational story elements. Indeed, nothing in the already sensational career of Hazel Farris was quite so spectacular as her manner of quitting it. Notorious in life as the victim of excessive passion, she was to become famous in death as a natural human wonder.

Legend has it that on the bright and shiny morning of August 6, 1905, a beautiful young housewife in Louisville, Kentucky, asked her husband for one new hat too many. The couple's heated argument grew into a tussle. Hazel Farris grabbed a pistol from a nearby bureau and fired. Her husband fell to the floor, dead.

The shot was heard by three passing policemen on their way to the station house in the vicinity. They burst in on Hazel Farris, still standing over her husband's body. She fired again until there were four dead bodies piled on the floor.

Outside, a crowd started to form. Beginning to realize what she had done, a frightened Hazel sought to hide in the house. Meanwhile, someone had summoned a deputy sheriff, who now cautiously entered by the back door in an attempt to take Hazel by surprise. But his stealth was no match for her reflexes or deadly marksmanship. As they struggled, his revolver shot off Hazel's ring finger. Nonetheless, she fired her fifth bullet of the morning to end the deputy's life.

By this time a large crowd had gathered on the premises. In all the excitement, Hazel managed to escape by the back door and through an alleyway. Evading armed pursuers, she fled Kentucky forever. Although a five-hundred dollar reward was posted in several states, police efforts to find Hazel Farris remained futile.

In 1906, at the age of twenty-six, the fugitive from justice with a price on her lovely head turned up in Bessemer, Alabama, hoping to begin a new life there. At this point, accounts of Hazel's life and death vary according to the teller of the tale. Narrators are about evenly divided on whether she moved into a boarding house to take up the role of a demure Bessemer schoolmarm, or set herself up as the madam of the best brothel in Jefferson County's red light district. (All that remains today of its two-story wooden structures is an empty field.)

Property of Luther Brooks

Hazel Farris, in her early twenties, at the turn of the century.

At the turn of the century, the new industrial town of Bessemer is said to have sported as many as thirty-two bars on a single street, whiskey being distributed from tank cars on side tracks to proprieters who bottled it under their own names.

Accounts of Hazel's life-style reconvene on two matters. Guilt, remorse, anxiety, or all three had turned Hazel into a heavy whiskey drinker (in secret if she were passing for a schoolmarm).

Moreover, Hazel Farris, wanted for the murders of five men, four of them officers of the law, ironically fell in love with a Bessemer policeman. Perhaps, as it is said, she needed to confide in someone;

perhaps whiskey loosened her tongue; or perhaps it was her intention to prevent secrets of the past from marring her future wedded happiness. In any event, Hazel Farris told the story of her past to the man she loved.

Whether out of moral indignation, devotion to duty, or interest in the five-hundred dollar reward—as variously speculated—Hazel's fiancé went directly to inform the authorities about her. Aware of her imminent arrest, Hazel withdrew to her room. Over a bottle of whiskey she made her decision not to submit to arrest. She took her own life by ingesting poison—arsenic or strychnine, the very chemicals that once were used as embalming fluids (before such use was made illegal in order to keep poison murders from going undetected).

Bessemer in the early 1900s had no morticians, no funeral parlors, no embalmment, and certainly no refrigerated morgue. Preparation for burial in that time and place consisted of nothing more sophisticated than the washing of a corpse with camphor. Hazel's remains were carried to a furniture store (still standing today) which sold caskets, there to await claim by next of kin or, if necessity dictated, a pauper's burial.

Almost everyone in Bessemer was intrigued by reports that the body of a beautiful dark-haired woman, who had shot five men and then killed herself, was laid out in A_____ and V_____'s furniture store. So folks began lining up to get a look at Hazel, the physically lovely murderess—but quickly, before the inevitable onset of decomposition. Mr. A_____, who had, after all, donated the coffin and the camphor, thought it only good business to charge a dime a look—at least for the next few days.

Inexplicably, however, and much to his surprise, most of the usual signs of physical deterioration were not occurring. Instead, loss of fluids reduced the one hundred six pounds of Hazel's five-foot, two-inch frame to a mere thirty-seven pounds. Hazel's body had somehow dehydrated to enter a state of mummification!

Part of the fun of tracking a legend is to gather narrative details from different sources and to make note of these variations. Historical preservationist James Walker has talked with many of the old-timers in Bessemer, who remember when Hazel was on display very early. All such witnesses agree on Hazel's great beauty, by late Victorian standards; but no two memories quite correspond on specifics, for instance, her attire. *You will find a different Hazel every time,* notes Jim.

In accordance with one version, having earned a tidy sum displaying Hazel, the furniture storekeeper decided to give his brother in Tuscaloosa a chance to do likewise. Mr. A_____ loaded Hazel's remains aboard a boxcar and wired his brother to expect her. There she was placed in the back of the C_____ store, where she remained on display for a year or two, until one Dr. Orlando C. Brooks, a traveling carnival man came through town.

Recognizing a promising carnival attraction, Brooks purchased Hazel the mummy for twenty-five dollars. Discrepancies between dates, even from one source, are par for the course of a legend; on or about May 20, 1907, without questioning Brooks's motives, the county authorities permitted him to claim the body. Luther Brooks, Orlando's great nephew, gives this account handed down within his family:

When Uncle 'Lando first got Hazel, he brought her to Nashville in 1906. He put her in the garage at my Granddaddy's house. And he went to Louisville, Kentucky, and stayed up there for five years, researching to see if she had any relatives. He didn't find any at all. So that's when he came back to Nashville and started showing Hazel. I think he was on Church Street when he first showed her. It was twelve days, and he showed her to eighteen thousand people.

For almost forty years, O.C. Brooks traveled with Hazel, exhibiting her all over the South, indeed all over the country and, according to some accounts, even before the crowned heads of Europe. Those who say Hazel was shown in Europe place O.C. Brooks with P.T. Barnum for a short time prior to World War II.

Dr. Brooks's exhibit was simple to produce. All he needed were some handbills, a tent, Hazel in her box, and a hairbrush and some fingernail clippers—the latter because Hazel's hair and fingernails continued to grow for almost thirty years. Brooks's handbill referred to Hazel's "beautiful suit of long, flowing hair."

There is considerable variation in the narrative details concerning

Hazel's years on the carnival circuit with O.C. Brooks. One representative version is as follows: naturally, so many years of being transported about made Hazel liable to minor mishaps. A gold tooth disappeared one night in Louisiana. Later on, after a journalist had written that if you touch the right hand of pistol-packing Hazel, the murderess of Kentucky, you will have good luck the rest of your days, Dr. Brooks decided to put on what used to be called an "after show."

He began charging an extra quarter, after the lecture, for the privilege of coming forward to rub Hazel's hand for luck. As a result of all that wear, the skeletal structure of her hand became exposed. She remained intact in most other respects, except for the disappearance of the little finger on her left hand (next to the damaged ring finger). Hazel was probably dropped in transit more than once, and the finger could have broken off during such an accident. Or perhaps that finger was deliberately broken off by someone who reckoned it would bring a greater share of good fortune than rubbing her hand. Luther Brooks recalls:

When I was in the carnival business, I would run into old carnies that knew Hazel and Uncle 'Lando back then. They told me how Uncle 'Lando would set his tent up and then he wouldn't even put Hazel in there the first three nights they were open. He would go through the midway, walking and telling about Hazel all the time—just building up their curiosity to see [adopting a barker's tone] "Hazel-one-of-the-wonders-of-the-world; Hazel-defying-every-law-of-nature." And then on Fridays and Saturdays, he'd open up. That means he didn't have to work but two nights, see. That was one of Uncle 'Lando's hypes. It all goes back to hype, you know, the way you make people want to see something.

According to several oral accounts (at some variance with Luther Brooks's), World War II put an end to the big time international circuses and further opportunities to show Hazel in Europe with the likes of P.T. Barnum's outfit. O. C. Brooks traveled less frequently now and only in the South. He eventually retired to the vicinity of Baton Rouge, Louisiana, after making well over two million dollars from showing Hazel around the world. The irony is that Brooks was penniless by the time he retired. He had spent money quickly, as quickly as he made it. In one of his letters he presumably wrote, "It's my way of being happy."

Brooks died in 1950, bequeathing Hazel to his twelve-year-old nephew, who drove down to Louisiana with his father in the family station wagon to pick up Hazel. They arrived to find that O.C. Brooks's quarters consisted of a one-room shack. All that was left of his millions were some posters about Hazel on the walls, and her traveling case, atop which Brooks had made his bed.

At first, the family could not find Hazel, but a search produced her case under Brooks's bed. Inside it was Hazel and in one much circulated version, a will, often "quoted" to this effect:

> This is Hazel. Take good care of her as I have not. I've shown her as a freak and I realize now that that is not what she is. She must be one of a kind and she is yours. Never sell her or show her as a freak and never bury her. Hazel must pay for her errors, and I must pay for mine. If you ever show her, you must donate all the money to charity; for I did not, and it should be in the name of science and education, for Hazel is a medical wonder.

And young Mr. Brooks never showed her as a freak, never sold her, never buried her, and showed her only to help raise money to build at least five churches across the state of Tennessee.

Luther Brooks, a native Nashvillian, good-humoredly denies that there was a will, that his uncle ever treated Hazel as a freak, and that he, Luther Brooks, now a successful businessman, ever did raise any money for charity when he showed Hazel himself. According to Brooks:

They had buried Uncle 'Lando the day before we got there. But you know, Uncle 'Lando made a lot of money. He died poor, though—the poorest. He always told everybody in my family that he was going to spend his money if he made it. He drank most of it up. During the Depression, Uncle 'Lando made one hundred and fifty a week. We've got partial records of where he would make this money.

He was charging a nickel a person to see Hazel. He'd stop on street corners, just anywhere, and show Hazel for a nickel a shot. He made as much as two hundred and thirty, forty dollars a week, during the Depression! But he worked at it. If he didn't drink his money up and gamble it, I don't know what he done with it; because he was the poorest of the poor.

There is one element impossible to overlook in that body of historical or situational data which provides the collector with clues that here indeed is credibility enough for legendry. That is the solid fact of Exhibit A, the mummified human body to which the legendary history (*biography* would be too limited a term here) of Hazel Farris is attached. By any name, the mummy exists. However, familiarity makes it impossible not to think of her as "Hazel," and almost prompts the fond tongue-in-cheek insistence that Hazel is "alive and well and living" in Nashville.

Over a cola at his spacious home on the outskirts of Nashville, Luther relates, seriously:

Before my dad died, he told me that I could have her. He didn't care nothing about it; didn't want to put her anywhere else, so I could just keep her in the family. I'll just pass her down.

Accounts of audience response to public showings of Hazel have also become matter for oral circulation. In the 1970s, to raise funds for the Bessemer Hall of History, she has been shown in a special "tote case," a satin cloth wrapped about her loins, a lecturer presiding at every moment.

At first, many adults approach Hazel with slight apprehension. Children are usually enthusiastic viewers from the start, though. Some folks find Hazel grotesque, most find her amazing, all who come to see her are somehow fascinated. Some few, perhaps with a sense of the poetic, are able to perceive a strange beauty about Hazel Farris in repose. In any event, the lecturers' relaxed manner and even affectionate attitude toward their exhibit soon put audiences at ease.

James Walker recalls that during such a scientific-educational exhibit:

A city bus driver heard us tell the part about how it was believed that if you rubbed Hazel's hand, you would ever live in prosperity and happiness. And thereafter, each day, he stopped by and rubbed her hand for luck. Later he told us that he was sure his life had been totally changed for the better. I don't know about the prosperity, but he's no longer a bus driver; he's gone on to higher things.

Luther Brooks and James Walker give respective accounts of having presided over special showings that would give physicians and embalmers a chance to "scrutinize" Hazel (the independent word choice of each). Indeed, Orlando Brooks as early as 1911 is alleged to have stated on his handbill that "the exhibitors will pay $500 in cash to anyone who will examine the body of 'Hazel, the Mummy' and prove that it is not genuine. This is a bona fide business proposition, made in good faith and without reserve whatsoever." For a second time in the story five hundred dollars was riding on Hazel. This time, however, no one is said to have collected.

Even though neither O.C. nor Luther Brooks would ever grant anyone permission to perform an autopsy, all professional scientists who have seen her have allegedly agreed that they were viewing a human body. None could explain Hazel's state of preservation beyond conjecturing that the chemical composition of her own body together with a massive intake of alcohol and a massive dose of poison combined to induce rapid dehydration.

Is Hazel really one of a kind? James Walker has heard about other mummies also associated with notorious backgrounds; but he believes they were embalmed, unclaimed bodies:

What makes Hazel's story different is that Hazel was never embalmed per se. Her organs were never removed. She does have all of her organs, her eyelashes, her teeth. I think Hazel is the only one of her type. There are some in the Smithsonian that are called incubated mummies, kept under glass; but Hazel has always been kept and shown out in the open.

I wish that Hazel could be put in a beautiful place and shown so that dust and stuff wouldn't get on her, and I think she'll be here for generations to come as an important part of science.

In the process of tracking this legend, one person, picture, or printed source led to another, until even Hazel herself had become included as a "resource person." A compilation of oral versions recorded from half a dozen informants is responsible for the density of narrative detail. There's no telling what further looking and listening may bring. Even now, narrative specifics extend to as many as four Southern states, while references to travel imply a much wider range of settings.

Ma Rainey II, "Well Blessed"

Knowing that circumstances will soon place you in Memphis, Tennessee, for example, perhaps you contact a friend there, who writes you back: "Listen, there is a little night place in Memphis called 'Blues Alley.' It has the old-timers, black musicians from Beale Street years ago, who are now sixty, seventy, or eighty years old. They are the *real musicians.* One big old woman named Ma Rainey II sings the blues there. She is raunchy, soulful, terrific. You won't want to miss her." And maybe, on impulse, you get in touch with Memphis Ma Rainey herself, to learn that she'll be happy to talk to you.

It's too noisy at the club for that; so she'll see you at her place an hour or two before she has to go to work, if you don't mind giving her a lift to the club. The next thing you know, you and your friend in Memphis, at ease in a small walk-up apartment, are engaging Miss Rainey in conversation so animated that content alone, none of the spirit, bespeaks a first encounter.

You ask her to tell you about herself, how she became involved in the blues scene.

I was born in 1906 in Columbia, Tennessee. Went to Nashville when I was four years old and run away when I was fourteen. There were thirteen of us kids. I'm the oldest. My father was a pastor. They have the worst children in the world [said laughingly]. I don't know where I got this blues singing at. My people was church people. I was the roustabout of the family.

I used to tell them I was going to run off. At thirteen I did. I joined up with a minstrel show. They called that a medicine show. Used to sell medicine at a dollar a bottle. It cured everything; didn't care what you had. They caught me up there and my mother like to tore me to pieces. OK, I joined up with the Sanctified Church—they call it the "Holy Roller." Anywhere there was a piano and that music was going I was right there. And they got me again.

My mother had taken sick. That's when they kept lookin' for me. I thought I had gotten cheated terrible because I couldn't get out and follow the blues. When my mother got kind of well, when I was fourteen, that was it. I joined up with the shows. I'm a comedian and a blues singer.

What was her name at birth, and what is her relationship to the late, great classic blues singer best remembered during the twenties, for whom this Ma Rainey is apparently named?

My real name is Lilly Mae Glover. I used to work for the old Ma Rainey. That's where I got the name. I used to work for a carnival show. Ma Rainey was in that. Ma Rainey used to get high all the time, you know, so her husband—he wasn't her husband, you know—hired me to sing. I had a voice then. And I would sing for old Ma Rainey. A lot of people used to think Ma Rainey was my mother. I said, "My mother never knowed nothin' about no blues."

This man named me "Baby Ma Rainey." I begged him to let me do comedy for him. He said, "You can't do comedy." I said, "I betcha I can." And I made me a suit, you know, great big old checkerboard overalls, a great big old white cap, and I had the bow go like the pants, and my shirt. I had my tennies on the wrong foot with the bows. We was playing some big fair in Jackson, Mississippi. So he said, "I'm gonna let you do comedy. What do you think about it?" The people were screaming. They didn't know what I was—a man, a girl—I was very young then, you know. They loved me. So he said, "From now on, you do comedy and the blues; you don't get the chorus no more."

What about her audiences then and now?

In those days a lot of the people in the audience were black. They led them in and sat them in the back. Black, white, it don't make any difference. All of them responds to me; and ever since I've been in the business, I've been pretty lucky. I tell the people, "We're all here together, to let it all hang out and have a good time." If someone isn't very nice and says things, I'll say,

Marshal Hagler

"A lot of people don't think I'll be seventy-one years old. The other night when I wasn't at work, Mr. Paul called me and said, 'Did you know that they're getting up and walking out because you're not here?' Yeah, I love this business, all right."

"Right back at you, Jack! Right back at you! Now, I come from Beale Street, it's true enough. But I'm going to treat you nice, and I know you're going to treat me nice." And they'll finally shut up after I straighten it out, you know.

Remembering what Johnny Shines said, you'd like to know how she thinks young people relate to the blues?

They used to didn't know what the blues was, honey. I used

*to tell the boys that was playin', "We're doin' blues tonight—
just plain old blues." They'd say, "Ma Rainey, we really don't
know nothing about no blues." I said, "Well, you're going to
have to learn. This whoopin' and hollerin' that y'all are carrying
on ain't going to work."*

*I went to see a friend of mine, and he was singing rock and
roll. He would sing, "Tell you, Baby, I'm* going! I'm going!"
*And he hollered that for about half an hour. I said, "Wherever
that b———'s going, I wish he'd go ahead on." And that kind
of fed me up on rock and roll. I like to do sweet melodies, but I
can't do 'em with just anybody.*

How does she feel about her life in the blues scene, looking back
on it now?

*Yeah, I love this business, all right, but it's kinda getting the
best of the old lady now. I've been sick about twenty-five years.
I think I'm holding up pretty good. I'm a diabetic, high blood,
hypertension, nerves. I've been crazy all my life. My eyes are
cataracted. Everything, you know, that anybody else ain't got, I
got it. I think I'm doing wonderful.*

*I'm satisfied with my life. I'm well-blessed. And the main
thing that keeps me going is the people. Do you know, I
haven't any kin person here, never did since I been here off and
on ever since '28?* But the apartment is full of tokens of friendship,
like Mother's Day cards, from caring fans.

*I've got the church fussin' at me as though I was a stray dog
about comin' to church. I say, "Ain't no use coming here today,
seeing how I'm going to sing the blues tonight."*

The church still considers the blues sinful, according to Ma
Rainey. Yet, to her way of thinking, all the music sung in black
churches sounds like blues. She misses the "old, slow hymns" she
says they used to sing, and adds, critically:

*They don't even preach in church no more till you pay 'em
off. I've seen them get happy in church when they sing. When I
sing in these clubs and things, I get happy, too. Look like it do
something to you, gets all over you, especially when you got a
good band working for you. Yeah, [chuckling] it do something
to you.*

Does she sing the famous first Ma Rainey's songs? Where does her material come from?

I didn't learn too much from Ma Rainey number one. I was working young, and she stayed too high. I have a friend that used to write, but mostly I like to do other people's numbers. I like this Memphis Slim. He's a great friend of mine. We used to run together. He's the one that wrote "Everyday I Have the Blues," and he give it to Count Basie. Count Basie didn't do much with it; B.B. couldn't do nothing with it. Wasn't nobody but Ma Rainey, number two, that could sing it.

I remember Slim used to work up and down Beale Street, and another fellow named Willie Ford. He was a drummer, I was a blues singer—I weighed one thirty-five then. Every Monday we had Blue Monday. We had a nice time, you know, and go play from one joint to the other. We'd have our Blue Monday; and while they were talking to the man, I'd cop the whiskey from over behind the counter [hearty laughter].

I remember when maybe we'd make three dollars. I have made thirty-five and forty cents a night. And now you can't hardly get me to come into a place and sing one song; it's gonna cost you fifty dollars. That just shows you. Of course, it takes money to live now. I buy a lot of clothes. She is wearing a long, turquoise gown for her performance this evening. *I try to keep myself up, you know.* Next to her bed in the combination living-bedroom is a carefully arranged display of all manner of cosmetics. Ma Rainey, who can't get around on her swollen legs very well, confesses, *Every day I turn around gettin' something from Avon. They bring it to me. I buy my wigs from them too."* She is generously perfumed; the scent, like her laughter, fills the room.

She likes it better now that times have changed. *Yeah, because you get paid for what you're doing. I remember the time me and B.B. used to work, and we used to come down to a place they called "Hamburger Heaven." You'd get dime hamburgers, three-cent coffee, and two-cent doughnuts. You was really living!*

She describes her own brand of blues as . . . *low-down blues:*

When you're drunk and getting it down and don't give a damn what's happening; this is deep in there, and we gonna get rid of this thing, understand—I don't see nothing for us to do but get rid of it—you got the blues. Some say, "Yeah, yeah, when your girlfriend puts you down." I say, "That ain't no blues. When I get into this heah poker game, and we have ten dollars raised; I lose my rent money, and I ain't got nothin' but the blues!"

In the car, on the way to Blues Alley, Ma Rainey plays a cassette recording of her music: *"I love you, baby, loved you from the start,/ You know, but you broke my heart./ Got my motor workin', Got my motor workin',/ Got my motor workin, But it just don't work on you.* She talks over the sound filling the automobile: *We going down the mighty Beale Street, honey. I used to be from one end to the other. I was wild. You couldn't tell it now, but I was young once upon a time. I used to run up and down here; I wouldn't know how to catch a bus now. This used to be all clubs.*

Dimly lighted W.C. Handy Park slips by the window. *This is where they have the festival every year. It's in summertime, when the weather is warm. I've been to St. Paul, Minnesota; Minneapolis, Minnesota; Texas, Kentucky, New York, Washington, and Tennessee. I've been to Germany. I went to Europe about three years ago. I didn't want to come back home. They were wild about me. It was kind of like what you call a festival.*

The car pulls up at the back entrance to Blues Alley. *I play from nine-thirty till 2 A.M. When that band's working right, look like it do something to you.*

Ma Rainey's rarin' to go.

How many saints is here tonight? Inside Blues Alley, a salt-and-pepper crowd enjoy the two house specialties, barbecued ribs and continuous blues. The black-white ratio is probably forty-sixty—the former, without exception, well-dressed and over thirty-five; the latter made up of collegiate, blue and white collar, or tourist types. Couples, led in as replacements for those departing, are seated at half-occupied tables for four to murmur hasty, first name introductions as short-lived acquaintanceships are struck between tablemates.

Backing one another up during solos or playing egalitarian instrumental roles, are seven musicians, all from the area, none of whom—according to the proprietor—could find regular gigs before Blues Alley opened. Actually, it reopened. Burned to the ground at its original location on November 6th at Street Alley, it was relocated six months later (six months during which eighteen musicians were out of steady work) to its present Front Street address on Cotton Row. If proprietor Paul Savarin continues to have his way, he'll relocate Blues Alley one more time before he's satisfied—to Beale Street, so all the Blues Alley musicians can return to their traditional home.

Tonight it's Rudy Williams on horn and doing the announcing; L.T. Lewis, the drummer with a gravelly, Satchmo voice; gold-toothed Booker T. Lowry at the piano; Johnny Moses on guitar; Sidney Montgomery on tenor sax, looking a little like Rosie Grier; Evelyn Young, in a no-nonsense denim pants suit, oblivious to the impact on audiences of an outstanding female alto sax player; and Sonny "Harmonica" Blake from West Memphis, Mississippi, trim in plaid wash-and-wear pants with matching tam, doing traditional material like "Little girl, you can plainly see,/ If you don't keep yoh hands out'f my pocket,/ I'll have to set you free."

Then, *I'm Ma Rainey, number two.* She introduces herself to a packed house, from the slightly raised musicians' platform. You notice that she is seated in a green padded, wooden armchair placed front and center. *I'm seventy-one years old, never had enough of lovin'.* Her syllables become spondees: *And it's too damned late now!* There are screams of laughter from the audience.

They got that thing they call "shake your booty"! Ain't that something? "Shake your booty!" Well, don't worry about me, 'cause all they gotta do is touch me, and the booty's already shook, darlin'.

She makes an oblique dedication to her two interviewers of a couple of hours ago and sings "Everyday I Have the Blues." As she sings, her years fall away. The seventy-one-year-old face becomes elastic, smooth, young. The voice is strong and true, obedient to her commands. The graceful, expressive fingers move unconsciously.

The rest is showmanship no longer in need of rehearsals. Ma Rainey stands, raises her turquoise skirt thigh high; and for thirty seconds, on edema-swollen legs, she dances like a young girl to whistles, cheers, and encouraging applause.

Halfway into her act, over wall-to-wall crowd noise, Ma Rainey begins her version of a traditional pitch:

I see some Saints in here. I'm gonna write a few of 'em off. And some of them's gonna write me off. We gonna get together on this, you know. I want to get old tryin' to get to see Salt Pepper—Saint Peter. Is that what it is? I thought it was Salt Pepper [They laugh; she's got their attention]. But, anyhow, I'm gonna do this number. When I enter the Golden Gates, boy, I'm gonna drink up all the corn there is up there [appreciative "all rights" from the crowd]. If Saint Peter sees me comin' up there with this jug like this [A gallon jar sits on the platform by Ma Rainey's left foot], he'll speak to me: "Who is that comin' up here with that empty jug?" [More good-natured laughter.]

"It's Ma Rainey!"

"Oh, that old Ma Rainey, who's down there on Beale Street?"

"Yeah, that's her."

"Tell her to go on back down there; she ain't got nothin'!" [Voluminous laughter from the crowd].

So, we gonna do this number, and while we do this number, I wanna see saints come over here. [Shouting now] I want to see how many saints is here tonight! Hold up your hands! All right, prove it to me, baby.

They prove it. While she sings "When the Saints Go Marching In," backed up by half a dozen musicians drawing out the number for ten minutes or so, the Blues Alley saints come marching forward, coins dropping, bills floating down into the huge glass jar. Reverently, though much less stiffly than in church, they come forward, one by one, many folks improvising a little dance in front of the "no dancing, please" sign stenciled on the largest drum.

Feeling good, Ma Rainey and the band practically blow the roof off to their "Kansas City Blues." Mid-song, Ma Rainey seems to forget herself. She leans way back in her stiff armchair, until her entire body is suggestively prone. She sits back up, still swaying, almost dancing seated. She looks suddenly graceful and chaste again. It comes as a shock, when her stint is over, that she has to be helped out of her seat and down off the platform.

Marshal Hagler

"I like to see my house look pretty fair, you know?" Ma Rainey II explains that blues musicians today can earn a better living than ever before. Memphis resident Karen Beth Mael holds the tape recorder while the out-of-town collector snaps pictures.

Epilogue

For the collector the most important benefits transcend the artifacts, photographs, note cards, and tapes. The best part is your realization that down home goodness, caring, self-sufficiency, sharing, wit, and unlimited talent are alive and well and living in the hearts of those folks from whom you collect traditional memories, music, laughter, song, and dance. You count yourself fortunate just to have had a reason to meet them.

But you also have fun, pure and simple: As in finding out to your wonder, upon testing your first witching wand (dowsing rod), that the blessed thing does inexplicably move in your hands and point to where you know there's water. As in riding your first muledrawn wagon over uneven farmland (and thanking your lucky stars you don't have to do this every day) to a strawberry patch (planted on the upside of the moon) and being invited to pick and eat all the luscious, bright red, big-as-plums berries you can hold.

Fun, as in getting ready to snap a picture of a man selling baskets off his wagon during a trade day in the Appalachian foothills, only to see through your camera lens just as you depress the shutter that, in a split-second feat of timing, the fun-loving merchant has reached into his wagon, whipped out—and is now holding up—an enormous pair of overalls. The photograph you made turns out to be one of your finest, and you never tire of telling friends how it happened.

You'll have encounters with folks so fine they're "all wool and a yard wide." Like Ida Thrasher, eighty-one-year-old grandmother of fourteen, who earns her living spinning wool in Mountain View, Arkansas. Who wouldn't respond instantly to a person who holds out her arthritic hands and tells you, "It don't hurt too bad. The more I use my hands, the better it is. I don't have time to do much knitting, but I knit socks when I watch TV."

Marshal Hagler

"My great grandfather in Mountain View made this spinning wheel out of black walnut." Ida Thrasher has been spinning "since I was about knee high to a duck. I grew up with my mother weavin' and everything."

You'll make new friends, who make you feel welcome as an eighty-degree day in January each time you come round to visit, who'll share their lives—their humor, their heartaches, and their cooking—with you, all because you're a folklore collector, which means someone who shows enthusiasm for the things they most love to do. Take white-haired Bill Livers (pronounced to rhyme with *divers*), with whom it's impossible not to strike an instant rapport:

William Livers: *They call me Bill for a short name. I tell you, I've been all over the country, but there ain't no place like Kentucky; ain't no place like Owenton. I live at Owenton.*

For longer than half a century this elderly black gentleman has been an accomplished old-time, Kentucky-style fiddler. At the age of twenty-three, to make sure there'd be no embarrassment, he secretly taught himself to play a friend's fiddle. Even the friend didn't know until Bill played "Old Kentucky Home" for him:

It took me almost a year to learn, and I haven't learned real good yet. I learned left-handed, and sometimes I get a little drunk and want to go back left-handed again.

Neither the excellent young white music makers who call their group the Bill Livers String Ensemble in his honor nor Bill's loving Kentucky fans pay any mind to the deafness which, nowadays, keeps him from knowing when his fiddle sometimes slips out of tune.

All my people is dead—my father, mother, stepfather, three sisters, and brother. All of them passed away but me. Sometimes I cry, but I don't do bad, don't aim to. I try to do a lot of good for a lot of people.

I reckon I've got them all over the country, and some of them I don't even know—they just know my name and my playing. They say I sure play well. If you can't enjoy your people, what are you going to do? I don't want to lose none [of my friends]. I just want to make them.

Well, he sure can count on one more, you think to yourself.

I'm having my fish fry Saturday. Last year I think I had close to a hundred people there—fish, hush puppies, coleslaw, potato salad, and Wild Turkey whiskey and cold beer, and some good country music. That's hard to beat. Could you come to it?

I caught most of the fish myself. I'm a great fisherman. Do you do much fishing?

You may find yourself developing an ear attuned to regional speech sounds and bits of domestic wisdom, as in the experience of this young adult who turned to folklore as an antidote to culture shock:

When we first moved to Alabama, our whole family [except my father, a native Alabamian] had to get used to a new culture. We could just understand the natives if we listened closely. It took me a while to learn to distinguish between "taters" and "arsh taters" [sweet potatoes and Irish potatoes]. To my father all this was old hat. As soon as we got here Daddy turned country farmer. My father's face takes on a proud glow whenever sweet potatoes are mentioned. Last year he grew some really prize-winning tubers. There was plenty to last the winter, but he couldn't store them in any shed because there just wasn't room. My aunt Gerterie suggested that Daddy store them the way Grandma did: Pile up a low mound of dry dirt, put the potatoes on top, then pile a couple inches of hay on the potatoes, then a good layer of dirt over all. The ones in the mound kept all winter, but we had a few in the cupboard, so we wouldn't have to go dig any up for a while, and they all rotted in a couple of weeks.

Perhaps, most importantly, you'll acquire a new sense of pride in grassroots heritage. If you did happen to grow up with an ash hopper for soap-making behind a house your father or grandfather literally built with his own two hands; if you spend leisure hours at home while your wife quilts and you whittle chains from solid blocks of wood—with independently movable links, sometimes double or even triple—you'll soon quit thinking in terms of "That's nothing; everybody I've known all my life can do that." Or "Well, I never had many of the advantages of kids today, like a car, plenty of spending money, and a college education. I just had to do the best I could."

You'll want to show others younger than yourself how to do some of the things you know about that they don't, before those skills become lost arts. You'll realize the worth of your traditional know-how, especially in relation to young folks you meet who wish they knew how to keep busy, wish they could get some real satisfaction, wish they could find "meaningful" work despite college degrees.

Walt Whitman wrote in 1885 that America is the only nation in the world where the head of state takes his hat off to the man in the street as well as the other way around. "The United States themselves are essentially the greatest poem," said this nineteenth-century poet, adding, "The genius of the United States is . . . always most in the common people." America is undergoing a re-awakening to such grassroots values as once celebrated by Whitman, though now particularly as these values thrive in the culture of the South.

But it really doesn't matter where you come from or what you do. Black, white; old, young; country or city dweller; rich, poor; lonely, sociable; outgoing or self-contained—by collecting folklore, documenting grassroots experiences, you will harvest their satisfactions as well as keep them alive for others.

The grass is healthy, the fields so green. I'm going for the time of my life. You come, too.

Classification Outline

The purpose of this outline is to help the amateur collector organize a file of eight genres of verbal and partly verbal folklore—short and long. Each section designated by a Roman numeral represents a different genre or type and should be treated as self-contained. That's because we cannot always apply the same patterned principles of classification to different kinds of verbal lore. Some types are classifiable according to their structure and their content, while others, like superstitions, are classifiable primarily by thematic content. Thus when referring to this classification, keep in mind that each major head contains its own pattern which is not necessarily consistent in form with other major heads.

Each section of the outline is designed in such a way that the letters and numerals may serve as a classification code. Select those letters and numerals—as many but no more than you need—and place them side by side in ranked alphabetical-numerical order, with a period between any two. For instance, unless you know from experience that a particular dialect pronunciation (I.C.) you collect is regional, you needn't apply the subset 1. But if, on the other hand, you know that "FIGMO" circulates in military folk groups, you will classify this acronym as *I.E.2.d.(a) (Folk dialect; Abbreviations; Occupational; Reference to behavior; Military).*

Why a code is helpful: Verbal labels are convenient and instantly recognizable. But a classification code becomes a necessity in a growing collection of verbal folklore. Without it, items that share similarities but also feature differences are too difficult to arrange consistently in a file. Take, for example, "If an owl hoots in the daytime, there will be a death in the family within a month." Obviously, this is a superstition, or folk belief—category V of this outline.

But what do you file it under next? Where do you place it in relation to other, perhaps similar, beliefs already in your collection? You need a specific place for this card. Like many superstitions, the example just given includes more than one topic. Here, the relevant subjects are animals (owl), death, and time (in the morning; a month). Rather than trying to decide now whether the owl or death is the more important subject (and later, when you might want to file a similar item, trying to remember what your decision was), you would best identify all topics in numerical order, filing this card accordingly.

Thus, the preceding belief might be classified *V.11.13.21*. (See V. Superstitions.) A variant of this belief, such as "A hooting owl means a death in the family," would be classified *V.11.13*. The absence of the 21—once you become familiar with the code—would immediately tell you the nature of the variation.

Often there might be more than one way to classify an item. So don't become anxious about "doing it right." Right is what common sense tells you to do. Just be consistent. For instance, take a charm like "bread and butter!" which is sometimes said by one of two people walking together if they are briefly forced apart by an obstacle like a light post, tree, or handrail. You could classify such an item as a charm, IV.A.2.h (Folk rhymes, etc.; Oral; Functional; Charms) or even as a proverbial phrase, II.B (Proverbial sayings; Phrase).

Classifying can be quite simple. Just hang on to your key, and you'll never have to memorize the system. As you need them, create and insert you own subsets, for example, occupations other than those listed under 2 in the folk dialect section (I). Where subsets leave off, file items alphabetically by key terms or by other means consistently used.

Short Forms of Verbal (and Partly Verbal) Folklore

I. Folk Dialect Vocabulary

    A. Nonstandard word forms (morphological variations), e.g., *holp* instead of *hélped*

    B. Nonstandard word combinations (syntactical variations), e.g., *might could* instead of *might be able to*, or *like to* ("I like to died") instead of *nearly*

    C. Nonstandard word sounds (dialect pronunciations), e.g., *modern* pronounced *modren*, or *mischievous* pronounced to rhyme with *devious*, or *washing* pronounced *warshing*

    D. Nicknames

E. Abbreviations spelled aloud or uttered as single words (acronyms), e.g., A.S.A.P. instead of *as soon as possible*

    NOTE: Use any appropriate combination (even no combination at all) of subsets, or create additional ones as needed: first, from 1-5 to identify the source folk group when known; second, from a-d to identify the referent, e.g., *Indian giver* may be classified as I.D.3.a (Folk Dialect; Nicknames; Ethnic; Reference to person); and, finally, from (a) through (e), or (z), as necessary, to identify a specific occupational group.

    1. Regional
    2. Occupational, e.g.:
        (a) Military
        (b) Prison
        (c) Academe
        (d) Architecture
        (e) Farming
    3. Ethnic (pertaining to national, religious, racial, or sex-related minorities)
    4. Age-related (prevalent within folk groups characterized by a particular age in the human life cycle)
    5. Confined to family or other very small folk group
        a. With reference to person(s)
        b. With reference to place(s)
        c. With reference to thing(s), e.g., food, clothing, tools, toys, parts of the body, furniture, etc.
        d. With reference to behavior, situation(s), or conditions(s)

II. Proverbial Sayings

    NOTE: The following pairs of subsets may be used whenever deemed appropriate:

    1. Parody
    2. Ethnic slur
        a. With puns or other wordplay
        b. Containing taboo (off-color, earthy, obscene) language

A. True proverbs (traditional whole statements, which rarely vary), e.g., "He who hesitates is lost"; or "Look before you leap."

B. Proverbial phrases (traditional metaphors, which vary in grammatical structure according to how they are incorporated into sentences; can often be recorded as "*to* phrases" e.g., "to make hay while the sun shines," or "to put the cart before the horse"

C. Proverbial comparisions (traditional similes), e.g., "like white on rice," "too wet to plow," or "cool as a moose"

D. Slam sayings (proverbial insults, retorts, wise cracks), e.g., "Keep your shirt on"; "Go take a long walk on a short pier."

E. Euphemisms (traditional understatements substituting for direct references), e.g., "It's snowing down South" instead of "Your slip is showing"; or to "kick the bucket" instead of "die"

F. Proverbial dialogue (traditional, often humorous exchange by formula), e.g., question: "Do you think the rain'll hurt the rhubarb"; answer: "Not if it's in tin cans."

G. Definition jokes, e.g., "Mixed emotions are seeing your mother-in-law drive off a cliff in your brand new Cadillac."

   NOTE: H-N, all literary or media parodies, all based on wordplay, need never be classified with subsets 1 or a; but an item such as "You can't have your Kate and Edith too" would be classified as II.A.1.a. (Proverbial saying; True proverbs; Parody; Puns or wordplay.)

H. Wellerisms

   (1) Complete, e.g., "'It won't be long now,' said the monkey as the train ran over his tail."

   (2) Partial, e.g., "'Not baad,' said the shepherd."

I. Tom Swifties

J. "She was only . . . ," e.g., "She was only the graphmaker's daughter, but she knew where to draw the line."

K. "Confucius say, '. . . . ' "

L. "Meanwhile, back at the ranch. . . . "

M. Authors and titles

N. Records and artists

III. **Riddles and Verbal Puzzles**

A. Oral

   1. True riddles (oldest forms; implied questions based on elaborate metaphors), e.g., "Humpty Dumpty"

   2. Riddling questions (traditional questions with unpredictable answers, though not impossible), e.g., "What has four wheels and flies?" (A garbage truck)

   3. Puzzle or problem (mind teaser which can be solved by ratiocination), e.g., "How much dirt is in a hole two and a half feet wide by three feet deep?" (None, silly; there's no dirt in a hole!)

4. Conundrum (based on homonymic wordplay)
5. Catch question ("loaded question"; any reply would be embarrassing to the respondant)
6. Pretended obscene riddle (answer is innocent)
7. Riddle joke (modern form; uttered for the sake of eliciting laughter rather than challenging the intelligence of the listener)
   a. Moron
   b. Elephant
   c. Other animals
   d. Celebrity (e.g., "What's yellow and rides a white horse?"—The Lone Banana)
   e. Food
   f. Color
   g. Ethnic
   h. "Sick"
   i. Knock-knock
   j. What did the_____say to the_____?
8. Tongue twisters
   (1) Intended obscene
B. Non-oral
   1. Gestures (accompanied by query, "What's this?")
   2. Drawings (usually "droodles" to identify)
   3. Palindromes (read the same forwards and backwards)
   4. All-letter sentences
   5. Over-and-under sentences
   6. Mnemonic devices (aids to the memory)

IV. Folk Rhymes, Poetry, Unrhymed Verse

NOTE: Use final subsets (a), (b), and/or (c) with any classification, as applicable.
(a) Parody (satirical, irreverent, or otherwise humorous take-off)
(b) Nonsense
(c) Circular
A. Oral
   1. Just for fun
      a. Nursery rhymes, e.g., Mother Goose
      b. Limericks
   2. Functional
      a. Play rhymes, e.g., "This little piggy went to market"

       b. Game rhymes, e.g., "Red Rover, Red Rover, let_____ come over"

         (1) Counting out rhymes

         (2) Jump rope rhymes

         (3) Ball bouncing rhymes

       c. Spelling rhymes

       d. Rhymes of derision, insult, retort

       e. Athletic cheers

       f. Work rhymes (occupational), e.g.:

         (1) Peddler's (street) cries

         (2) Planting rhymes

         (3) Military cadence chants

       g. Belief rhymes, e.g., "Homely at the cradle / Pretty at the table"

       h. Charms, e.g., "Sty, sty, leave my eye / Go to the next one passing by"

       i. Prayer rhymes

       j. Toasts

    3. Topical comment

       a. Commemorative

       b. Full length parodies

B. Graphic

    1. Inscriptions (on objects, e.g., flyleaf, powder horn)

    2. Autographs

    3. Epitaphs

    4. Graffiti (wall, desktop)

       a. Scatological

       b. Sexual

       c. Political

       d. Religious (or sacrilegious)

       e. Ethnic (minorities)

       f. Lovelorn or romantic

       g. Gossip (about celebrities, literary characters, or lesser known figures)

       h. Slams (derision, insults, responses to injury)

       i. Group rivalry (fraternal organizations, athletics, etc.)

       j. Literary (quotations, misquotations, allusions)

       k. Advertising

       l. Musings (miscellaneous banter or philosophy)

       m. Miscellaneous slogans

n. Booze, drugs, etc.

o. I.D. (identification by name, initials, etc.), e.g., "Kilroy was here"

p. Novelty (pictorial or graphically innovative)

V. Superstitions—Folk Beliefs

NOTE: Topic headings without preceding capital letters are included for the convenience of the collector in identifying beliefs by sections. The capital letters have been omitted to save unnecessary steps in coding, permitting the collector to classify "If an owl hoots in the daytime, there will be a death in the family within a month," for example, as *V.11.13.21 (Superstitions; Death; Animals; Times, etc.)* instead of *V.A.11.B.13.C.21. (Remember, capital letters are omitted in the following outline.)*

Human Life Cycle, Rites of Passage

1. Birth, infancy, childhood
2. Human body
   a. Physical features as indexes of character traits, e.g., long second toe indicates dominant personality
   b. Sensory phenomena, e.g., significance of nose itching, ear ringing, chill, etc.
   c. Personal grooming
   d. Reproduction
3. Folk medicine, e.g., as collected:

a. Remedies	(1) Burns
b. Cures	(2) Hiccoughs
c. Preventive measures	(3) Insect stings
	(4) Pain of childbirth
	(5) Rheumatism
	(6) Stomachache
	(7) Warts

4. Home, domestic pursuits, e.g.:
   a. Food, eating, drinking
   b. Clothing
   c. Housekeeping
5. Economic and social relations, e.g.:
   a. Prosperity
   b. Friends

      c. Occupations and pastimes
         (1) Theatrical
         (2) Nautical
         (3) Gambling
  6. Travel and communications
  7. Love, courtship, marriage
  8. Dreams
  9. Gestures, actions, e.g., knocking wood, whistling
10. Accidents, mishaps, e.g., finding, dropping, breaking, tripping over an object, etc.
11. Death and funereal customs

Nature and Environment

12. Weather
13. Animals and animal husbandry (care, feeding, cures, etc.)
14. Fishing and hunting
15. Plants and plant husbandry
16. Insects
17. Fire
18. Sites and settings
19. Colors

Cosmic Phenomena

20. Heavenly bodies
21. Times, numbers, seasons, special days

The Supernatural

22. Witchcraft, clairvoyance, ghosts, magical practices

Miscellaneous, e.g.:

23. Wishing and luck (in general)
24. Explanatory beliefs. e.g., Alabama soil is red from the blood of Confederate soldiers.
25. Collectibles, e.g., cigarette packages, labels, etc. (if amassed will, for instance, provide free guide dogs for the blind)
26. Refutation of factual reports, e.g., John F. Kennedy is really still alive; the moon landing is a hoax; etc.

Long Forms of Verbal (and Partly Verbal) Folklore

NOTE: All numerals and letters preceding classification categories for long forms are cumulative in each of the remaining sections. This device should make it possible for the collector to use any subset with any major category, as applicable to what is actually collected. For patterns of structure and theme are less predictable in long forms than short forms of verbal folklore.

VI. Legends (Belief Tales)

A. Religious
   1. Saints' legends
   2. Stories of miracles, revelations, answers to prayers, etc.
   3. Bible of the folk
B. Supernatural
   4. Memorates (first-person accounts of supernatural signs, magic, the marvelous)
   5. Revenants (ghosts—those who return temporarily)
   6. Urban belief tales
C. Personal legends
   7. Hero legends
   8. First-person reminiscences and family stories (collectively, family saga)
   9. Anecdotes
      a. About famous individuals
      b. About local characters
D. Local legends and migratory legends
   10. Of specific places
      c. Of names (how derived—folk etymology)
      d. Of geographic features
      e. Of man-made structures
   11. Historical
      f. Associated with periods of time or historical milestones
      g. Of sensational events
      h. Associated with regional politics
   12. Occupational
      NOTE: Specify as necessary, beginning with i.

VII. Folktales

A. Animal tales (animals behaving like people), e.g.: "The Three

Little Pigs''
1. Explanatory, e.g., how the woodpecker came by its coloring
2. Moral (fables), e.g., the fox and the sour grapes
B. Ordinary folktales, e.g., *Maerchen,* such as "Cinderella," collected by the Brothers Grimm; Jack tales
C. Cante fables (narratives in which songs are embedded)
D. Picture stories
E. Humorous stories
    3. Formula tales
        (A) Cumulative tales (chains), e.g., "The House that Jack Built," "Good News/Bad News"
        (B) Catch tales (in which the narrator tricks the listener into asking a question, the answer to which causes the latter embarrassment)
        (C) Endless tales (narrative pattern of endless repetition)
    4. Tall tales (windies)
    5. Modern jokes and joke cycles, e.g.:
        (1) Numbskull stories (noodle tales), e.g., marking the boat to identify fishing site
        (2) Married couples
        (3) Traveling salesmen
        (4) Children's misunderstandings
        (5) Drunks
        (6) Wind-up dolls
        (8) Shaggy dog
          NOTE: Use any of the following subcategories when appropriate:
          (a) Religious themes and stereotypes
          (b) Ethnic (racial, national) themes and stereotypes
          (c) Masculine/feminine stereotypes
          (d) Sexual themes
          (e) Patriotic themes
          (f) Involving wordplay
          (g) Told in dialect

VIII. Folk Songs

NOTE: The two undesignated major headings are unnecessary to the coding process but may be helpful to the collector in making identifications.

Near-songs

A. Wordless, e.g.:
          (a) Chin music
          (b) Yodeling
B. Talking, e.g.:
          (a) Talking blues
          (b) Square dance calls
          (c) Auctioneers' chants
          (d) Some game rhymes

True songs

C. Functional, e.g.:
          (a) Lullabies
          (b) Work songs
          (c) Play, game, or dramatic dance songs
          (d) Mnemonic songs
D. Narrative (including ballads)
E. Lyrical
    1. Folk lyrics (expressing a mood; secondarily narrative), e.g.,
       Negro blues; "On Top of Old Smokey"
    2. Spirituals, religious songs
    3. Homiletic songs (giving advice, preaching)
    4. Gamblers, drinkers, ramblers, prisoners
    5. Regional, occupational
       NOTE: Use as appropriate, especially with E.1-5.
       a. Youth
          (1) Nursery
          (2) Elementary school
          (3) Camp
          (4) High school
          (5) College
       b. Humorous
          (6) Parody
          (7) Nonsense
          (8) Dialect
       c. With formularized gestures

Suggestions For Further Reading

Not only may folklore be enjoyed popularly and recreationally, but it may be studied as a serious discipline or in conjunction with various other disciplines. Folklore is thus attended by all the special, general, theoretical, and practical scholarly and popular literature which accompanies any internationally established area of study having multiple specialties and approaches. A bibliography adequately reflecting the possibilities for further reading in just those areas of folklore that have been touched on in the present book would require a separate volume.

In an attempt to appeal to a diversity of interests, a mere sampling of reference works, periodicals, special collections, and guides is provided here. The list which follows is eclectic to say the least—a potpourri, the sole purpose of which is to enable you to get started in any number of directions. In turn, its limitations are compensated for by the excellent bibliographies contained in the majority of the works that are listed.

Aarne, Antti. *The Types of the Folk-Tale, A Classification and Bibliography*. Trans. and ed. Stith Thompson. 2nd ed. Folklore Fellows Communications, No. 184. Helsinki: Suomalainen Tiedeakatemia, 1961.

Ben-Amos, Dan, ed. *Folklore Genres*. Austin: University of Texas Press, 1976.

Bluestein, Gene. *The Voice of the Folk: Folklore and Literary Theory*. Amherst: University of Massachusetts Press, 1972.

Boatright, Mody C. *Folklore of the Oil Industry*. Dallas: Southern Methodist University Press, 1963.

Boatright, Mody C.; Downs, Robert B.; and Flanagan, John T. *The Family Saga and Other Phases of American Folklore*. Urbana, IL: University of Illinois Press, 1958.

Brunvand, Jan Harold. *Folklore: A Study and Research Guide*. New York: St. Martin's Press, 1976.

Brunvand, Jan Harold. *The Study of American Folklore: An Introduction*. 2nd ed. New York: W.W. Norton & Company, Inc., 1978.

Calendar of Festivals. The National Council for the Traditional Arts, Inc., 1346 Connecticut Avenue, N.W., No. 1118, Washington, DC 20036.

Center for Southern Folklore Newsletter. Center for Southern Folklore, 1216 Peabody Avenue, P.O. Box 4081, Memphis, Tennessee 38104.

Coffin, Tristram Potter, ed. *Our Living Traditions: An Introduction to American Folklore*. New York: Basic Books, 1968.

Coffin, Tristram P. and Cohen, Hennig. *Folklore in America*. Garden City, NY: Doubleday, 1966.

Coffin, Tristram Potter and Cohen, Hennig, eds. *Folklore from the Working Folk of America*. Garden City, NY: Doubleday, 1973.

The Devil's Box. Tennessee Valley Old-Time Fiddlers Association, Route 4, Madison, Alabama 35758.

Dorson, Richard M. *America in Legend: Folklore from the Colonial Period to the Present*. New York: Pantheon Books of Random House, 1973.

Dorson, Richard M. *American Folklore*. Chicago: University of Chicago Press, 1959.

Dorson, Richard M. *Buying the Wind: Regional Folklore in the United States*. Chicago: University of Chicago Press, 1964.

Dorson, Richard M. *Folklore and Fakelore*. Cambridge, MA: Harvard University Press, 1976.

Dundes, Alan, ed. *The Study of Folklore*. Englewood Cliffs, NJ: Prentice-Hall, Inc., 1965.

Dundes, Alan, and Pagter, Carl R., comps. *Urban Folklore from the Paperwork Empire*. Austin: University of Texas Press for the American Folklore Society, 1975.

Folklore Women's Communication. P.O. Box 5653, Santa Fe, New Mexico 87502.

Glassie, Henry. *Pattern in the Material Folk Culture of the Eastern United States*. Philadelphia: University of Pennsylvania Press, 1968.

Goldstein, Kenneth S. *A Guide for Field Workers in Folklore*. Memoirs of the American Folklore Society, Vol. 52. Hatboro, PA: Folklore Associates, 1964.

Hand, Wayland, ed. *American Folk Legend: A Symposium*. Berkeley: University of California Press, 1971.

Hand, Wayland D., ed. *Popular Beliefs and Superstitions from North Carolina*, Vols. VI and VII of *The Frank C. Brown Collection of North Carolina Folklore. 7 vols*. Durham, NC: Duke University Press, 1961-64.

Hyatt, Harry W. *Hoodoo—Conjuration—Witchcraft—Rootwork*. 4 vols. Hannibal, MO: Western Publishing Company, 1970–74.

Journal of American Folklore, 1888 f.

Keil, Charles. *Urban Blues*. Chicago: University of Chicago Press, 1966.

Kentucky Folklore Record, 1955 f.

Knapp, Mary, and Knapp, Herbert. *One Potato, Two Potato . . . : The Secret Education of American Children*. New York: W.W. Norton & Company, Inc., 1976.

Laws, G. Malcolm. *Native American Balladry*. Rev. ed. Philadelphia: American Folklore Society, 1964.

Leach, Maria and Fried, Jerome, eds. *Standard Dictionary of Folklore, Mythology, and Legend*. 2 vols. New York: Funk and Wagnalls, 1949-50; rpt. and rev. in 1 vol., 1972.

Levine, Lawrence W. *Black Thought and Black Consciousness*. New York: Oxford University Press, 1977.

Lichtman, Allan J. *Your Family History: How to Use Oral History, Personal Family Archives, and Public Documents to Discover Your Heritage*. New York: Vintage Books of Random House, 1978.

Lipman, Jean, and Winchester, Alice. *The Flowering of American Folk Art, 1776-1876*. A Studio Book. New York: Viking Press in cooperation with the Whitney Museum of American Art, 1974.

Malone, Bill C. *Country Music U.S.A.: A Fifty-Year History*. Publications of the American Folklore Society, Memoir Series, Vol. 54. Austin: University of Texas Press, 1968.

Mid-South Folklore, 1973 f.

Mintz, Jerome R. *Legends of the Hasidim*. Chicago: University of Chicago Press, 1968.

Mississippi Folklore Register, 1967 f.

Montell, William Lynwood. *Ghosts along the Cumberland: Deathlore in the Kentucky Foothills*. Knoxville: University of Tennessee Press, 1975.

Montell, William Lynwood. *The Saga of Coe Ridge: A Study in Oral*

History. Knoxville: University of Tennessee Press, 1970.

Moore, Willard B. *Molokan Oral Tradition, Legends, and Memorates of an Ethnic Sect*. Berkeley: University of California Press, 1968.

North Carolina Folklore Journal, 1954 f.

Paredes, Americo, and Stekert, Ellen J., eds. *The Urban Experience and Folk Tradition*. Austin: University of Texas Press for the American Folklore Society, 1971.

Phillips, Karen, ed. *A Catalogue of the South*. Southern Living Books. Birmingham, AL: Oxmoor House, Inc., 1974.

Randolph, Vance. *We Always Lie to Strangers*. New York: Columbia University Press, 1951.

Reisner, Robert. *Graffiti: Two Thousand Years of Wall Writing*. Chicago: Cowles Book Company, Inc., 1971.

Ritchie, Jean. *The Dulcimer Book*. New York: Oak Publications, 1963.

Sandberg, Larry, and Weissman, Dick. *The Folk Music Sourcebook*. New York: Alfred A. Knopf, 1976.

Southern Folklore Quarterly, 1937 f.

Stern, Jane. *Trucker: A Portrait of the Last American Cowboy*. New York: McGraw-Hill Book Company, 1975.

Tennessee Folklore Society Bulletin, 1934 f.

Thompson, Stith, ed. *Motif-Index of Folk-Literature: A Classification of Narrative Elements in Folk-Tales, Ballads, Myths, Fables, Mediaeval Romances, Exempla, Fabliaux, Jest—Books and Local Legends*. 6 vols. Bloomington: Indiana University Press, 1955; rev. ed. Copenhagen: Rosenkilde and Bagger, 1955-58.

Toe Tappin-Talk. National Clogging and Hoedown Council, Route 1, Box 319, Seneca, South Carolina 29678.

Tullos, Allen, ed. *Long Journey Home: Folklife in the South*. Chapel Hill, NC: *Southern Exposure*, 1977.

Weitzman, David. *Underfoot: An Everyday Guide to Exploring the American Past*. New York: Charles Scribner's Sons, 1976.

Wilson, Eugene. *Alabama Folk House*. Montgomery: Alabama Historical Commission, 1975.

Yoder, Don, ed. *American Folklife*. Austin: University of Texas Press, 1975.